IMAGES
of America

HOTEL TYBEE

Longtime Tybee Island resident Jane Wheeler Shuman stands at Hotel Tybee's front entrance in 1945. (Courtesy of Jane Wheeler Shuman.)

ON THE COVER: Taken by Southern Photo Service of Savannah, Georgia, in 1946, this image was captured during a photograph shoot in the beachside courtyard of Hotel Tybee. The purpose of the photograph shoot was to gather images to be used in advertising Tybee Island—Savannah's beach—as a fun, seaside resort destination. Shown third from the right is Ann Daum Wilson. (Courtesy of Ann Daum Wilson.)

IMAGES
of America

HOTEL TYBEE

Harry George Spirides

ARCADIA
PUBLISHING

Published by Arcadia Publishing
Charleston, South Carolina

Library of Congress Control Number: 2012943977

For all general information, please contact Arcadia Publishing:
Telephone 843-853-2070
Fax 843-853-0044
E-mail sales@arcadiapublishing.com
For customer service and orders:
Toll-Free 1-888-313-2665

Visit us on the Internet at www.arcadiapublishing.com

*This book is dedicated to my late father, George, and my
mother, Frances, who worked for more than 40 years
in our family's hotel and restaurant business located on
the same land where Hotel Tybee once stood.*

CONTENTS

ACKNOWLEDGMENTS

I would like to thank the following people and organizations who assisted me in my research and/or provided the images that were selected to be featured in this book: Luciana Spracher (who makes historical and archival research look so easy—but it is not), Honey Ryan, Sarah Jones, Hank Buckley, Ann Daum Wilson, Jane Wheeler Shuman, Florence Spirides, Frances Spirides, Eugenia Spirides, Bill Bland, Mae Ricci, Kitty Hernandez, Lorton Livingston, Mary Friedman, Kathy Layne, John Duncan, Clair Price, Barbara Wright, Nickie Alexander, Nancy Byrd, Mary Frances Robertson, Jeanne Mills, Barry Paschal, Paula Branson, Linda Wittish, the Georgia Archives, the Georgia Historical Society, the Tybee Island Historical Society, the City of Savannah Municipal Archives, CMMI Architects, the Central of Georgia Railway Historical Society, Allen Tuten, Terry Michaud, Ed Mims, Les Winn, and Belinda DeLisser.

INTRODUCTION

Very few tourism- or hospitality-related historic structures remain on Tybee Island today to tell us about Tybee Island's early days as a bustling seaside resort destination. By telling the story of Hotel Tybee through this book, it is my hope that I will take readers on an informative journey through Tybee Island's long history of accommodating visitors and serving hospitality.

When I was a child, my family and I lived in a building that was the last remaining section of Hotel Tybee (its two-story north wing), which my father had purchased in 1967. Most of Hotel Tybee, which was originally built in 1889, had been demolished in 1961 by its previous owners. I literally grew up at that same hotel property. Today, it is known as Ocean Plaza Beach Resort. As a child, I was mesmerized by the stories about Hotel Tybee that my father told. In fact, when I was in third grade at Tybee Elementary School, I turned in a report on Hotel Tybee. I remember my teacher telling me that she was fascinated by my report, which earned me an A.

My family has been living on Tybee Island and managing businesses in its downtown commercial district for the past 70 years. A list of businesses on Tybee Island that we have operated over the years includes the Tybrisa Pavilion, Hotel Tybee, the world's first Days Inn, Ocean Terrace Motel (later known as the Sands Motel), Ocean Terrace Cottages, Veranda Motel & Restaurant, and the modern-day, 204-room Ocean Plaza Beach Resort along with its Dolphin Reef Oceanfront Restaurant & Lounge. Over the past 30-plus years, I have worked in every conceivable job at hotels, motels, and restaurants located on the land where Hotel Tybee once stood. Today, I am an owner and also chief executive officer of Ocean Plaza Beach Resort. I consider it an honor, a privilege, and also a solemn responsibility to be today's custodian of the legendary Hotel Tybee property.

This book is built upon a foundation of old Hotel Tybee brochures, photographs, and other memorabilia that was handed down to me by my 94-year-old great-aunt Florence Spirides whose husband was the last general manager of Hotel Tybee for several years before it was torn down. In 2007, as part of the city of Tybee Island's 120th anniversary celebration, I pulled together all these items to create a commemorative website outlining the history of Hotel Tybee. The website is located at www.HotelTybee.com. This website was so well received by many past and present Tybee Island residents that at their urging I decided to expand my Hotel Tybee memorabilia collection by conducting historical research and then write this book. I wanted to properly record for future generations to enjoy the lost history of this magnificent hotel, where, over the 72 years of its existence, hundreds of thousands of people vacationed with their loved ones and friends and created special memories that lasted a lifetime. Hundreds of conventions and other social events were also held at Hotel Tybee.

As a former US Coast Guard officer and a military veteran, I am paying my respects to the long military history of Tybee Island by donating my percentage of the profits from the sale of this book to the restoration of Fort Screven's Tybee Post Theater into a fully functioning community performing arts and cultural center. Located on the north end of Tybee Island, Fort Screven was a busy US Army installation at one time. Built in 1897 as a seacoast defense artillery installation, this fort was designed to defend the entrance to the strategic Savannah River and Port of Savannah. It also served as the headquarters and garrison of the US 8th Infantry as well as a military diving school. It was an active military installation from the Spanish-American War through World War II. Fort Screven was decommissioned in 1945 and sold to the City of Tybee Island, which was known at that time as the City of Savannah Beach. After Fort Screven was decommissioned, the Tybee Post Theater's attendance declined, and the building fell into ruin. As of today, the building has been partially restored thanks to the efforts of a fine group of volunteers known as the Friends of Tybee Theater. I encourage you to visit their website at www.TybeePostTheater.org to see how you can assist them in restoring the Tybee Post Theater.

Tybee Island's days as a popular seaside resort destination began with the grand vision of one very determined and talented man. That man was Capt. Daniel G. Purse. Daniel Gugle Purse was born in Savannah, Georgia, on November 14, 1839. He held the title of captain because he served as a captain in the Confederate States Army during the Civil War. He served his time under the command of Gen. J.F. Gilmer, chief of engineers in the Confederate service.

After the war, Daniel Purse served as a City of Savannah alderman for two consecutive terms in 1877–1879 and 1879–1881. In 1892, Purse led a project, which deepened the Savannah River channel from the city to the ocean. This provided the port with a lot more merchant shipping business by allowing larger ships to call on Savannah. Purse was the first president of Brush Electric Light and Power Company, a predecessor of Savannah Electric and Power Company, which was acquired by Georgia Power. Through his efforts, the city of Savannah became the first city in the world to entirely replace gas streetlights with electric lights.

Purse served Savannah through many endeavors: as president of the Savannah Board of Trade for 14 years, successively; as commissioner for Savannah's Bureau of Freight and Transportation during its five years existence; and as president of Savannah Bank and Trust Company.

Daniel Purse purchased a majority of Tybee Island in April 1885. Purse believed Tybee Island, which is located 12 miles east of Savannah, had great potential to be developed into a popular seaside beach resort destination comparable to the likes of New Jersey's Long Branch, Maryland's Eastern Shore, Rhode Island's Newport, and Massachusetts's Nantucket Island. Tybee Island was mostly uninhabited at the time, but because of its close proximity to the mainland, four miles of beautiful beaches, pristine waterways, exotic flora and fauna, pure artesian drinking water from shallow wells, and excellent storm water drainage, Purse believed Tybee Island had great potential to become one of the first publicly accessible beach resort destinations in the Southeast United States. He knew he had a very viable business concept in attracting Savannah residents and tourists to Tybee Island from near and far. For Tybee Island's new permanent residents, nearby Savannah afforded all the luxuries of a big city. However, Purse knew that the slow two-hour steamboat ride between Savannah on the mainland and Tybee Island was an obstacle preventing him from achieving his grand plan for Tybee Island's commercial development. He knew he needed to reduce the travel time between the two points to no more than 30 minutes. To do this, he established the Savannah & Tybee Railway Company and then connected these two cities with a railway line. When Purse proposed building his railroad across 12 miles of salt marsh to Tybee Island, he was met with a lot of public skepticism. Undaunted, in 1885, he and John C. Rowland purchased Deptford Plantation and Causton Bluff near Savannah and built a railway line from that point to Tybee Island. It began operation in 1887. Purse was president of the Savannah & Tybee Railway Company until the Central of Georgia Railway Company acquired it.

When the Savannah & Tybee Railway Company successfully completed its Savannah-to-Tybee railway line, the availability of such quick transportation to and from Savannah that summer resulted in a record 80,000 people visiting Tybee Island in a four-month period. On numerous occasions that summer, hundreds of visitors were unable to find lodging accommodations on Tybee Island, and many others were deterred from visiting the island due to this lack of accommodations. As a result, plans were drawn up for a large hotel to be built.

The Tybee Hotel Company was a corporation created in Chatham County, Georgia, on June 30, 1888. The incorporators included some of the wealthiest and most enterprising merchants of Savannah at that time. The original charter members and shareholders of the Tybee Hotel Company were a group of investors who were led by the president of Savannah National Bank, a Savannah city alderman, and future five-term mayor of the City of Savannah, Herman Myers, who served as its first president. The other original charter members were William Garrard, S. Guckenheimer, P.W. Meldrim, J.J. Dale, George A. Mercer, William Kehoe, R.E. Lester, J.P. Williams, R.G. Erwin, A.A. Solomons Jr., A.R. Lawton Jr., C.N. West, Andrew Hanley, F.G. duBignon, J.A. Einstein, R. Falligant, W.G. Cooper, Gazaway Hartridge, Samuel Meinhard, T.P. Ravenel, and W.B. Stillwell.

On February 3, 1889, general contractor Winton & Burgess was awarded the construction contract, and on February 15, work began on building Hotel Tybee near the south end of Tybee Island. A particular parcel of land had been purchased on which to build Hotel Tybee. The selected site is both adjacent to the Atlantic Ocean and also is one of the highest elevated parcels of land on the island, at 16 feet above sea level, which is a good attribute in case of flooding from a storm. The architects were L.B. Wheeler and A.S. Eichberg from Atlanta. Upon opening of the first Hotel Tybee, A.S. Eichberg remarked that the architectural style of the hotel was "Swiss Renaissance."

On August 29, 1889, when the construction of the first Hotel Tybee was completed, the *Savannah Morning News* reported the following:

> It has 120 guest rooms and thirty rooms for other purposes. The main building is 250 feet in length, and has a frontage on the beach of 205 feet. It has all the modern improvements of electric bells, speaking tubes, gas and water, bath rooms, etc., and stand pipes and hydrants for fire protection. The guests' rooms have, in addition to the usual doors, slat doors, so that the rooms can be private and at the same time have ample ventilation. Passages are left between the rooms so as to let the breeze pass through the rooms from whichever direction it may blow.
>
> In every respect the hotel is a model for a seaside resort, and the architects deserve credit for their successful effort in planning a building so admirably adapted for the purpose for which it is intended.
>
> The dining room is large, airy, and handsome. It is 126 feet by 46 feet which is 10 feet wider and 15 feet longer than that of the DeSoto Hotel in Savannah. Immediately adjoining it, and separated by double doors, is the carving room, and adjoining that is the kitchen and other rooms belonging to the culinary department. A bar and billiard room is also provided.

The building also featured a 12,000-gallon freshwater storage tank, artesian waterworks, and an outdoor covered pavilion for group meetings and dancing. It had a spacious rotunda and a half mile of open-air verandas, including a large observatory overlooking the island on its top floor.

On July 31, 1909, the first Hotel Tybee burned completely down to the ground in the middle of the night after a fire started in its electricity generation plant, spreading to the dining facility and then to the hotel and other buildings. All 100 hotel guests escaped safely; although, many guests lost valuable personal items.

Hotel Tybee was rebuilt bigger, stronger, and more magnificent than before. The second Hotel Tybee opened for business on June 1, 1911.

The second Hotel Tybee was built to be fireproof, using reinforced concrete-and-steel construction. Built in a Spanish Revival style of architecture, it was a beautifully designed structure. It directly faced the Atlantic Ocean, with wings expanded to catch the breeze at all hours. It was acknowledged by many leisure travel writers at the time to be one of the most charming seaside resort hotels in the country. As the years passed, more and more people discovered Hotel Tybee and stayed there, returning often.

Upon entering the hotel, either from the beach or from the railroad station or highway, the first impression made upon visitors was immediately pleasant and welcoming. Always receiving a gracious greeting from the doorman, the pervasive atmosphere of geniality, which was foreign to so many hotels at the time; the speedy attention given to all incoming travelers; the evident desire to have guests regard this not as a mere hotel but as their real home while at the seashore—these and many other features gave Hotel Tybee a special reputation as being the "South Atlantic's Favorite Resort."

The cool, spacious lobby, which had to one side the registration desk, was painted in refreshing colors and featured comfortable chairs to sink into with ease. A broad passageway took guests to the main dining room in the northern wing, where the pleasures of the palate were enhanced by the view of the breakers rolling onto the beach and the refreshing cool breeze borne over a thousand miles of ocean. Every meal was a delight in this room, with its quick and attentive service and its carefully prepared food that embraced everything each season had to offer. The chef was a skilled artist, and the kitchen and dining-room staff was well trained. An orchestra played the latest popular tunes and old favorites.

On this ground floor were the usual amenities of a first-class hotel, including a barber and beauty shop and a beach shop and snack bar, which featured a soft-drink fountain. A number of guest rooms were also located in the southern wing of this floor as was the convention center. The second, third, and fourth floors, reached by elevators, were dedicated to guest rooms. In all, the hotel had 110 guest rooms, which could be rented separately or in suites of two, three, or four bedrooms, with private baths. Liberal in size, with high ceilings, fans, and ample windows, the hotel as a whole was constructed to ensure perpetual ventilation of cool air. Its rooms were comfortable at all hours. In every bedroom was a telephone, and none was without its running artesian water. The hotel was entirely screened and always kept in immaculate condition by a corps of well-trained and supervised housekeepers.

Broad piazzas extended the length of the main section of the building, which was a favorite lounging place, and from them extended the long boardwalk to the hotel's beachside dancing and special event pavilion, the bathhouse, and the beach. There was nothing to break the view of the ocean from this famous boardwalk, and strolling along it was popular. The hotel owned and operated its own electric light plant and shallow-well artesian waterworks. The beachside Hotel Tybee dancing and special event pavilion and the Hotel Tybee Bathhouse, which had 300 rooms for men and 200 for women, were owned and operated by the hotel in order to maintain them according to the hotel's high standards. The hotel pavilion's 50-by-100-foot dance floor was always thronged with hotel guests and visitors at night, when popular six-piece orchestras furnished music.

Well-kept grounds surrounded the hotel. Its grass, flowers, and shrubbery added to the attractiveness of the building. A complete irrigation system frequently watered the foliage. Adjacent to the hotel were seven cottages, owned and operated by the hotel, which could be rented by families desiring greater privacy and space. These were comfortably furnished and were in high demand by those who intended to spend an extended amount of time at the seashore. Each had a little porch to add to the comfort of the occupants.

Hotel Tybee frequently won recognition as a popular convention place. From its earliest days, its reputation in this regard was very strong. Conventions of all sizes were eager to enjoy the island's many attractions and combine their business with the various pleasures offered by the resort. Every year, several prominent associations, corporations, government agencies, and other types of organizations returned to Hotel Tybee for their annual sessions, while others were being introduced to its charms for the first time.

For decades, the above synopsis of Hotel Tybee held true until February 1961, when Monroe Wrecking Company of Savannah, who had been hired by the owners of Hotel Tybee at that time, the Seaview Development Company, demolished a majority of the landmark Hotel Tybee. It then subdivided the land into smaller parcels and sold them off to interested buyers.

Over the past 45 years, my family has been acquiring these individual parcels of land in an attempt to reassemble the original Hotel Tybee tract of land so that we may preserve and enhance the tradition of accommodating visitors and serving hospitality as was first established there by Daniel Purse and Herman Myers some 125 years ago.

One

THE FIRST HOTEL TYBEE

1889–1909

Hotel Tybee's main building is shown in the middle of this 1898 photograph along with its rental cottages on the left and its dancing and special event pavilion on the right. All structures shown are constructed entirely of wood. The location is Fifteenth Street and Strand (on the Atlantic Ocean), Tybee Island, Georgia. (Courtesy of the Georgia Archives.)

This image is of a postcard, sent in 1910. It shows a man walking in a field just north of Hotel Tybee with its 20,000-gallon water tower in the foreground, which is located next to the kitchen's smokestack. The back of the postcard states the following: "Glimpse of Hotel Tybee. This is a famous seashore resort near the city of Savannah, popular in both winter and summer. A suburban railroad runs frequent trips to the island from Savannah. It lies at the mouth of the Savannah River, and Tybee Beach affords fine surf bathing." (Courtesy of John Duncan.)

This photograph features the entire east-facing, beachside profile of the original Hotel Tybee around 1898. From left to right, this photograph shows the rental cottages; the dancing and special event pavilion; Hotel Tybee; the picnic pavilion with individual, covered picnic tables appearing in front of it; and on the far right, a bathhouse with individual showers and bathing-suit changing rooms for men and women. Behind the bathhouse is located the servants' quarters and laundry building. (Author's collection.)

The father of Tybee Island's tourism and hospitality industry, this is an 1890 sketch of Capt. Daniel G. Purse, who, at one time, owned most of Tybee Island. He was born in Savannah in 1839 and served during the Civil War in the engineer corps of the Confederate States Army. Purse, who was an exceptional visionary, believed that Tybee had great potential to be developed into a popular seaside resort destination. Tybee was mostly uninhabited at the time and had no roads running to it. Purse knew that the slow two-hour steamboat ride between Savannah and Tybee was an obstacle preventing him from achieving his grand plan for Tybee's commercial development. He knew he needed to reduce the travel time between the two points to no more than 30 minutes, so he created the Savannah & Tybee Railway Company. When Purse completed the 18-mile-long Savannah-to-Tybee railway line in 1887, the availability of such quick railway transportation to and from Savannah that summer resulted in a record 80,000 people visiting Tybee Island in a four-month period. The stage had thus been set to build a "Mammoth Hotel." (Courtesy of the Georgia Historical Society.)

This is a postcard rendering of Hotel Tybee shortly after it opened for business in 1889. On July 15, 1902, Hotel Tybee's flagpole, located on top of the roof cupola, was struck by lightning during a severe thunderstorm. The lightning bolt started a fire in the cupola attic. The fire was quickly extinguished by the hotel fire brigade. No injuries were reported. (Courtesy of Linda Wittish.)

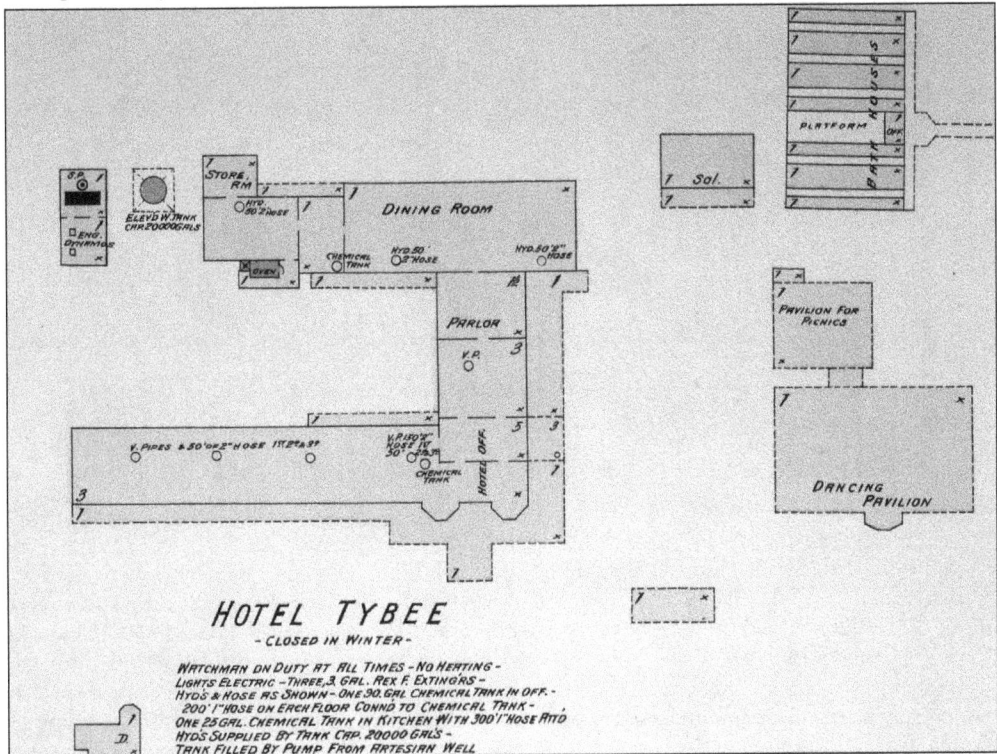

Above is an 1898 Sanborn Fire Insurance map of Hotel Tybee. It shows the layout of the resort at the time. Hotel Tybee hosted many conventions in its dancing pavilion, dining rooms, and parlor. Some of the conventions held there were those of the Georgia State Dental Association, Georgia State Association of Probate Judges, Georgia Agriculture Society, Georgia Bankers Association, Atlanta City Salesman Association, Georgia Association of Post Office Clerks, and Georgia Bar Association of lawyers. (Courtesy of the Chatham County Geographical Information System.)

HON. HERMAN MYERS, MAYOR.

Pictured is the father of Hotel Tybee. Building Hotel Tybee was the vision and work product of its founder Herman Myers, president of the Savannah National Bank and future five-term mayor of the City of Savannah. Above is a photograph of Herman Myers taken in 1900. He was born in Germany in 1847. When he was a child, his parents immigrated to the United States. He owned a tobacco and wool businesses in Savannah under the name H. Myers & Bro. He also was president of a cigar manufacturing business, El Modelo Cigar Manufacturing Company of Tampa, Florida, and then of the Cuban-American Cigar Manufacturing Company of Tampa and Havana, which he later merged with the El Modelo Company. After selling his interests in the tobacco industry, Myers organized the Savannah Grocery Company, a wholesale operation, and served as its president. In 1885, Herman Myers organized and became president of the National Bank of Savannah and served in that capacity until his death. Myers held a large interest in the Savannah & Tybee Railway Company and also Hotel Tybee. (Courtesy of the City of Savannah Municipal Archives, used with permission.)

16

This early photograph of Hotel Tybee's ocean-side profile was taken in 1894 shortly before J. Glascock Mays, superintendent of the Georgia division of the Southern Express Company, died after falling out of a third-floor window at Hotel Tybee at night. As seen above, the original Hotel Tybee was built at the edge of the beach. (Courtesy of the Georgia Archives.)

Savannah Morn[ing]

EXTRA!!   EXTRA!!

FLAMES SWEEP HOTEL TYBEE; HUNDRED GUESTS ESCAPE

FANNED BY WIND FROM OCEAN, BLAZE REDUCES BIG FRAME STRUCTURE TO ASHES.

Fire Starts in Power House, Works Its Way Through Kitchen and Dining Room and Soon Claims the Entire Structure.

SENATE VOTES TO OUST M'LENDON

HOUSE MAY FOLLOW SUIT.

EXAGGERATED EGO MAY DO FOR THAW

NEW PHASE IN THE CASE.

Above is a copy of the cover of the *Savannah Morning News* on July 31, 1909, announcing Hotel Tybee caught fire and burned to the ground. On February 11, 1910, Hotel Tybee majority-owner F. Bartow Stubbs announced that he would rebuild Hotel Tybee. He contributed the land plus $25,000 cash to the deal, and investors provided the balance of the $200,000 necessary to build a new Hotel Tybee. The proceeds from a fire insurance policy paid a small part of the construction cost. (Courtesy of the Tybee Island Historical Society.)

18

Two

THE SECOND HOTEL TYBEE

1911–1961

The above 1928 photograph shows Hotel Tybee's heavily landscaped driveway leading to a concrete patio at the front doors of the hotel's registration lobby. The hotel's characteristic red tile roof supported by architectural eave bracing and twin, five-story-tall bell towers impressed upon arriving guests that a unique experience awaits them. Extending from the front doors is a covered walkway to Hotel Tybee's train station. (Courtesy of the Georgia Historical Society.)

This photograph shows Hotel Tybee in 1911 shortly after its grand opening. On June 1, 1911, the second Hotel Tybee formally opened for business with a gala dinner at 8:30 p.m. among much celebration and fanfare. Invited to the dinner, which was hosted by proprietors F. Bartow Stubbs and Barney Cubbedge along with manager Arthur Walty, were the hotel directors, bondholders, and newspaper representatives as well as the general public. (Courtesy of Hank Buckley.)

This photograph shows Hotel Tybee from the ocean's edge in 1911, just shortly after its grand opening. Hotel Tybee's dancing and special event beach pavilion and its bathhouse are in the foreground. To the left of those structures is Durdan & Powers's beach pavilion, which later became known as the Breakers and then as the Brass Rail restaurant and nightclub. Hotel Tybee hosted many conventions and other special events in its beach pavilion. Some of the conventions held there were those of the Cottonseed Crushers' Association of Georgia, Georgia State Bankers Association, and Georgia Bar Association of lawyers. (Courtesy of the Georgia Historical Society.)

Mills B. Lane, the president of Citizens and Southern Bank, is seen here in his office around 1930. In 1910, he remarked that a magnificent new hotel on the Tybee coast would be of inestimable value to Savannah. Mills B. Lane was directly responsible for bringing together a group of investors to raise the funds necessary to build the second Hotel Tybee. He was also chairman of the Hotel Tybee Building Committee to oversee its construction. (Courtesy of the Georgia Historical Society.)

Mills B. Lane's photograph appeared on the cover of *Southern Citizens* magazine shortly after his death in August 1945. Mills B. Lane was born in Lowndes County, Georgia, in 1860. As its visionary president, he expanded Citizens and Southern Bank's presence in Georgia by establishing branches in Savannah, Augusta, Macon, Atlanta, Athens, and Valdosta. Not content with keeping Citizens and Southern a Georgia bank, Lane spread into South Carolina, opening branches in Charleston, Columbia, and Spartanburg. (Courtesy of the Georgia Historical Society.)

An unidentified man, woman, and child appear to be waiting for the next arriving train at Hotel Tybee's train station in this 1920 photograph. Until 1923, the only way to travel to Tybee Island was by steamship or railroad. (Courtesy of the Georgia Historical Society.)

This photograph shows Hotel Tybee (back left) in 1920 as one looks south from the intersection of Main Street (today's Butler Avenue) and Fourteenth Street. An electrical power generation plant is seen on the right side, and Hotel Tybee's train station, with railroad passenger cars parked near it, is in the middle of the photograph. (Courtesy of the Georgia Historical Society.)

Swimmers are seen here enjoying the surf at Tybee Island in 1919. The women are wearing the customary swimming attire of the day, which included black stockings. Each dress had small metal weights sewn into its hemline to keep it weighted down so no part of the dress would float upward while in the water. (Courtesy of the Georgia Archives.)

Shown climbing a tree in front of Hotel Tybee in 1918 are, from left to right, Mildred Browne Wheeler, Wilkie Browne, and an unidentified female. (Courtesy of Jane Shuman.)

This postcard of Hotel Tybee's dancing and special event beach pavilion was sent via US Mail in 1920. Hotel Tybee's main building is seen in the back left of this image. Tragically, on June 23, 1907, Jack Apple, a recent Georgia Tech college graduate, was paralyzed after diving headfirst into very shallow water from Hotel Tybee's beach pavilion. (Courtesy of an anonymous donor.)

The above photograph, which looks north from the intersection of Main Street (today's Butler Avenue) and Sixteenth Street (today's Tybrisa Street), was taken at the Tybee Island train depot shortly after Tybee Road opened on June 21, 1923, which subsequently allowed people with their beloved automobiles to travel freely to and from Tybee Island. The $1-million, 23-mile-long Tybee Road between Tybee Island and Savannah, with six steel-and-concrete bridges, was opened among

much celebration. The *Atlanta Constitution* newspaper sponsored an automobile caravan of 38 cars from Atlanta to Tybee Island via Augusta to celebrate the special occasion of the opening of "Georgia's first road to the sea." Many prominent citizens and politicians participated in the caravan and festivities. (Courtesy of Mary Friedman.)

This 1915 photograph of an unidentified group of men, women, and children was taken in front of Hotel Tybee's dancing and special event beach pavilion, which was located directly on the beach. At high tide many of the steps on which these people are seated were submerged by the Atlantic Ocean. Many group meetings, conventions, and other social events were held in this pavilion over the decades. (Courtesy of the Georgia Historical Society.)

As required by city ordinance, lifeguards were sponsored by Tybee Island's commercial beach pavilions, which included Tybrisa Amusement Center, Izlar's beach pavilion, and Tybee Beach Hotel (Hotel Tybee), to stand watch on the beach to keep swimmers safe. This photograph was taken sometime in the 1920s. Among others, on June 23, 1904, Hotel Tybee Orchestra violinist Arthur O'Neal drowned in the ocean in front of Hotel Tybee. He had recently relocated from Boston, Massachusetts. (Courtesy of Hank Buckley.)

Surf Bathing at Hotel Tybee, Tybee Island, Ga.

This postcard of people surf bathing at Hotel Tybee was sent via US Mail in 1911. Most people during that era rented their bathing suits from bathhouses located along the beach. These bathhouses provided bathers with room in which to change their clothes and use the restroom and shower. (Courtesy of an anonymous donor.)

Hotel Tybee's dancing and special event beach pavilion is featured on the right center of this 1925 photograph while the Breakers Restaurant and Dance Pavilion (later called the Brass Rail) is shown on the left. Shown in the foreground are people enjoying the beach with a lifeguard supervising in his stand. (Courtesy of the Georgia Historical Society.)

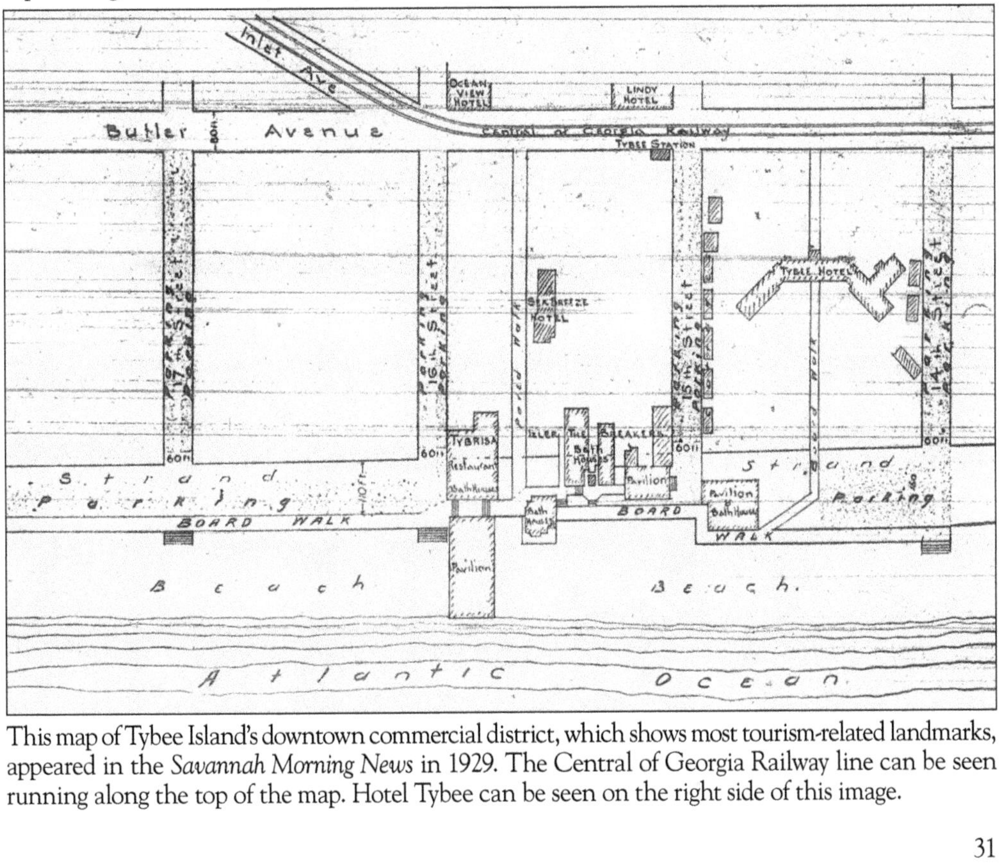

This map of Tybee Island's downtown commercial district, which shows most tourism-related landmarks, appeared in the *Savannah Morning News* in 1929. The Central of Georgia Railway line can be seen running along the top of the map. Hotel Tybee can be seen on the right side of this image.

Tybrisa Pavilion can be seen in the distance of this mid-1920s photograph, which was taken from the Hotel Tybee beach pavilion during a social event. On February 1, 1935, Hotel Tybee's dancing and special event beach pavilion was torn down after heavy northeast winds, during very high tides with crashing waves, seriously damaged the structure. (Courtesy of the Georgia Historical Society.)

Tybee Island's beach pavilions can be seen in this early-1930s photograph, taken from a boat offshore. Hotel Tybee is visible on the right side of the photograph behind its beach pavilion, with the Tybrisa Pavilion being located on the left side. (Courtesy of Hank Buckley.)

Above is a snapshot of Hotel Tybee taken in 1924 by Nan and Pearcy Bland of Statesboro, Georgia. (Courtesy of Bill Bland.)

Nan and Pearcy Bland (right) appear with a friend near Hotel Tybee's main entrance in this 1924 photograph. (Courtesy of Bill Bland.)

The Pajama Orchestra performs on the beach in front of Hotel Tybee in 1931. Big-name, touring musicians frequently performed at Hotel Tybee. (Courtesy of the Georgia Historical Society.)

People of all ages are seen walking and playing on the beach and in the surf south of Hotel Tybee's beach pavilion around 1925. (Courtesy of the Georgia Historical Society.)

Hotel Tybee can be seen in the background of this photograph, which was taken in the public parking lot located at the intersection of Fifteenth Street and the Strand. (Courtesy of the Georgia Historical Society.)

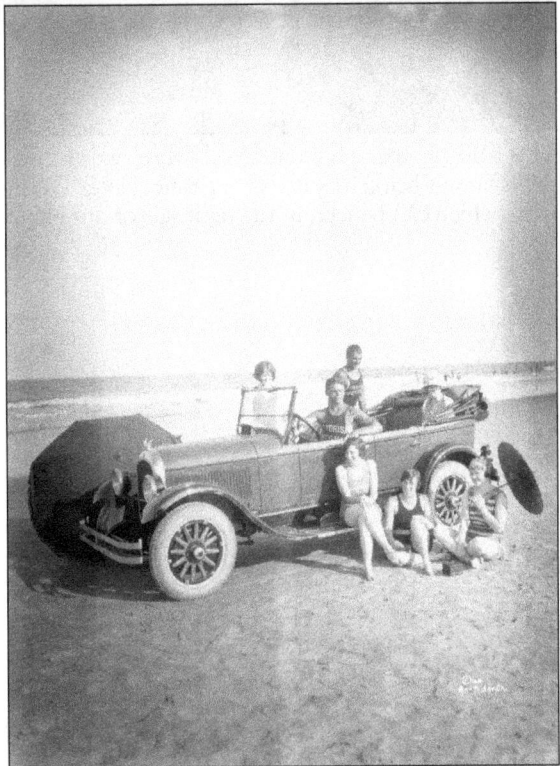

Taken to produce an advertisement for the nearby Tybrisa Amusement Center, this 1924 photograph shows a car on the beach with male and female models. (Courtesy of the Georgia Historical Society.)

This 1930s photograph shows Hotel Tybee's west-facing profile and its main entrance. It appears that the lawn was being irrigated at the time. Hotel Tybee's convention center was located in its south wing, which can be seen in the right side of this photograph. (Courtesy of Florence Spirides.)

Here, Hotel Tybee's Claude Mann Orchestra entertains hotel guests during the 1920s. Live music and dancing were always an integral part of Hotel Tybee's ambiance. (Courtesy of the Georgia Historical Society.)

This 1916 Sanborn Fire Insurance map of Hotel Tybee shows the layout of the entire city block. The driveway located above the hotel in this sketch is today's Fourteenth Street, and the driveway below the hotel is today's Fifteenth Street. Hotel Tybee's seven rental cottages plus servants' quarters appear along Fifteenth Street next to the Hotel Tybee beach pavilion. (Courtesy of Chatham County Geographical Information System.)

This photograph shows Hotel Tybee's registration lobby in 1939. This space provided guests with a place to meet and relax. It was located on the first floor of the main building. Gambling activities at times took place in a room adjacent to the registration lobby. Roulette wheels, poker tables, slot machines, and horseracing machines were available to those interested in participating. (Courtesy of the Georgia Historical Society.)

This photograph of the registration lobby appeared in a 1940s official Hotel Tybee brochure. The beach shop and snack bar, which is shown at the far side of the lobby, were always busy with guests purchasing souvenirs, beach supplies, snack food, drinks, and toiletry items. It was in the registration lobby that on May 31, 1924, Hotel Tybee manager and part-owner A. Lamar Poindexter was shot in the abdomen and killed by Bernard H. Rawls, a Hotel Tybee night clerk, after Rawls's employment at Hotel Tybee was terminated by Poindexter. Rawls was sentenced to life in prison for his crime. (Courtesy of Florence Spirides.)

This is Hotel Tybee's main dining room as it appeared in 1939. This room was located on the first floor of the hotel's north wing. The wide windows at the end of the dining room afforded a magnificent view of the beach. Many famous orchestras played here, as well as in the bar, at the beachside pavilion, and on the back patio. (Courtesy of the Georgia Historical Society.)

Above is a photograph of the main dining room that appeared in a 1940s official Hotel Tybee brochure. Unique murals of geese, clams, and oysters were painted on the walls. (Courtesy of Florence Spirides.)

Above is a photograph of Hotel Tybee's veranda dining room as it appeared in 1941. This room, which was actually a screened-in, outdoor patio, overlooked the hotel's beachside courtyard and also the Atlantic Ocean in the distance. (Courtesy of the Georgia Historical Society.)

Here is one room of Hotel Tybee's convention center as it appeared in 1941. On July 24, 1915, the Savannah Board of Trade hosted a meeting at Hotel Tybee, which was attended by the most prominent and wealthiest citizens of the state. The group established a Georgia branch of the Southern Settlement and Development Organization for the purpose of colonizing the approximately 11 million acres of idle farmlands of the state and to develop the state agriculturally. (Courtesy of the Georgia Historical Society.)

This photograph of a gathering held in Hotel Tybee's convention center appeared in a 1940s official Hotel Tybee brochure. On June 7, 1918, the Georgia Bar Association of lawyers held its annual convention in the same room. US Supreme Court Justice Beverly D. Evans and US senator J. Ham Lewis were speakers. (Courtesy of Florence Spirides.)

This photograph of the inside of the hotel's beach shop and snack bar appeared in a 1940s official Hotel Tybee brochure. (Courtesy of Florence Spirides.)

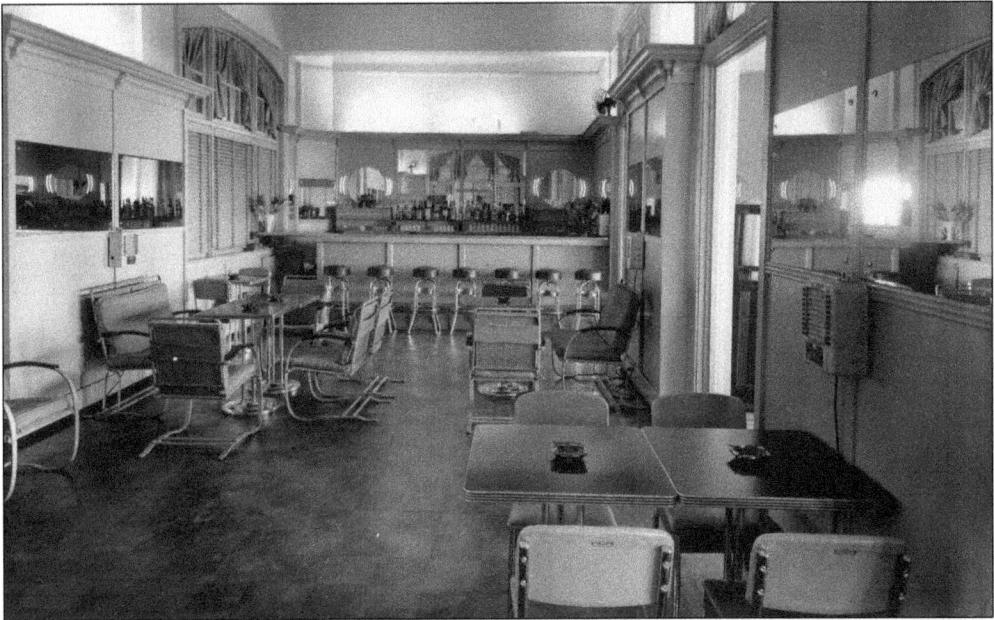

This photograph shows Hotel Tybee's bar in 1941. This bar was the center of Tybee Island's sizzling nightlife for many years. Nightly dancing and live music were almost always featured. On July 15, 1926, Hotel Tybee hosted a dance for the officers of the Georgia National Guard, 122nd Infantry Regiment from north Georgia, who were conducting their annual two-week training at Tybee Island. They thoroughly enjoyed the bar. (Courtesy of the Georgia Historical Society.)

Above is another photograph of the inside of Hotel Tybee's bar, which also appeared in a 1940s official Hotel Tybee brochure. On August 6, 1926, several members of the 121st Infantry Regiment of the Georgia National Guard enjoyed Hotel Tybee's bar too much and celebrated the closing of their annual summer two-week training camp by conducting a drunken riot and attacking Hotel Tybee. Soldiers broke windows, tore down doors, and heavily damaged Hotel Tybee property. (Courtesy of Florence Spirides.)

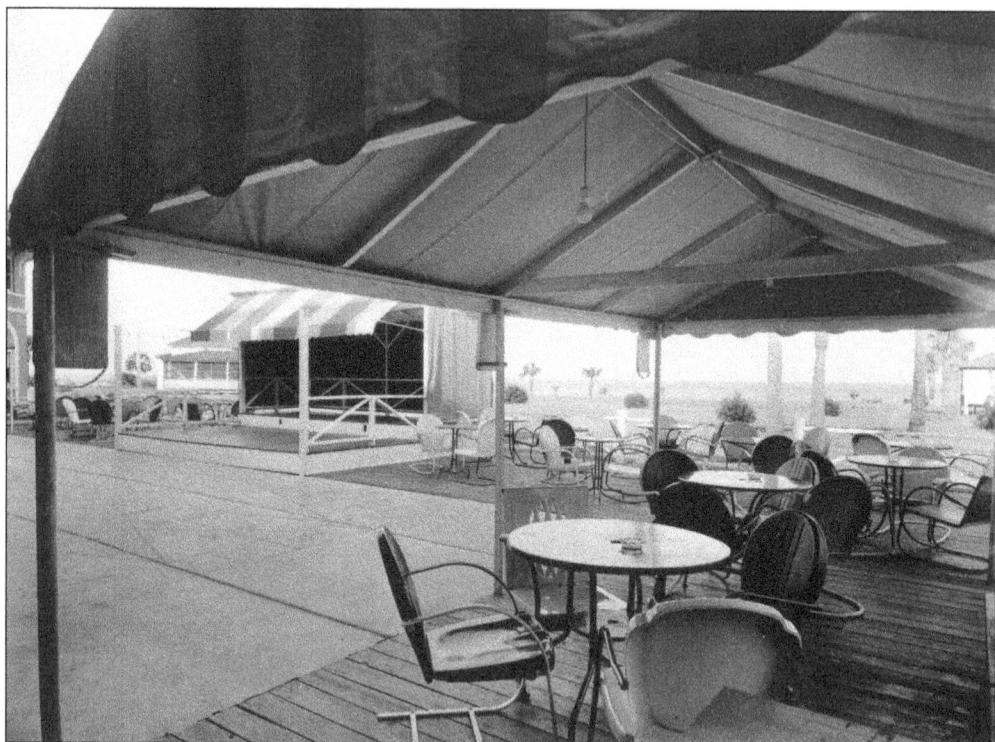

Hotel Tybee's beachfront patio was always the perfect place for moonlit dancing, cooled by ocean breezes. The bandstand and stage with the dance floor/shuffle-board deck can be seen on the left side of this 1941 photograph. The Atlantic Ocean can be seen on the right side. (Courtesy of the Georgia Historical Society.)

Above is a photograph of a dance being held on the beachfront patio, which also appeared in a 1940s official Hotel Tybee brochure. On September 2, 1927, the Delta Tau Delta fraternity, during its annual national convention, held a dinner and a dance for several hundred of its members at Hotel Tybee. (Courtesy of Florence Spirides.)

Hotel Tybee featured 110 hotel guest rooms. This 1941 photograph shows a typical guest room with one double-sized bed. In the 1940s, it cost $4 per night to rent this type of room. If one wanted a private bathtub or shower, the rental rate was $8 per night. (Courtesy of the Georgia Historical Society.)

Appearing in a 1940s official Hotel Tybee brochure was this photograph of a typical family bedroom with two double beds. This type of guest room even came with a telephone. In the 1940s, it cost $6 per night to rent this type of room. If one wanted a private bathtub or shower, the rental rate was $10–$12 per night. (Courtesy of Florence Spirides.)

Also featured in a 1940s official Hotel Tybee brochure was this photograph of a Hotel Tybee tower suite parlor. In the 1940s, it cost $15–$20 per night to rent a one-bedroom suite with an attached parlor–living room. (Courtesy of Florence Spirides.)

Views from Hotel Tybee's guest room windows were always quite stunning. This 1912 image shows such a view, looking toward the southwest past Hotel Tybee's adjacent rental cottages. Tybee Inlet, also known as the Back River, can be seen in the distance. (Courtesy of the Georgia Historical Society.)

This 1950s photograph was taken from one of Hotel Tybee's guest room windows. Looking toward the southeast, past Hotel Tybee's adjacent rental cottages, Tybrisa Amusement Center's two-story bathhouse, restaurant, and bowling alley building can be seen on the left side behind the Ferris wheel. In the distance is the Atlantic Ocean. (Courtesy of Florence Spirides.)

Above is an aerial photograph of Hotel Tybee that appeared in a 1940s official Hotel Tybee brochure. On the beach at every street and extending out into the ocean can be seen wooden jetties, which were used to prevent beach sand erosion. (Courtesy of Florence Spirides.)

Walter and Mary Boyd appear in this photograph that was taken in front of Hotel Tybee sometime during the 1920s. (Courtesy of the Tybee Island Historical Society.)

This photograph with Mary Boyd in it standing in front of Hotel Tybee in the 1920s appears to have been taken at the same time as the photograph on the opposite page. She appears to be holding a bouquet of flowers. The ornate details of Hotel Tybee's Spanish Revival architecture can be clearly seen in this photograph. The dramatic roof bracing underneath the eaves was a characteristic element of Hotel Tybee's architectural aesthetics as were the semicircular ground-floor window and door frame components. (Courtesy of the Tybee Island Historical Society.)

Ernest and Blanch Boyd appear in this photograph taken next to the Hotel Tybee train station in the 1920s. The west-facing profile of Hotel Tybee's main building as well as its north wing can be seen in the background. (Courtesy of the Tybee Island Historical Society.)

This 1920s postcard shows the ocean-side boardwalk that extended from Hotel Tybee to Hotel Tybee's dancing and special event beach pavilion. Rocking chairs and tables lined this promenade where unobstructed, panoramic views of the Atlantic Ocean were always present. It was a very popular place to relax, hang out, and breathe-in ocean fresh air. (Courtesy of the Georgia Historical Society.)

Joseph Wheeler (right) and friend Blue Bell Brinson pose in front of Hotel Tybee in 1930 shortly before they attended a banquet in Hotel Tybee's dining room. (Courtesy of Mae Ricci.)

A woman can be seen walking on the concrete walkway that ran from Hotel Tybee to the corner of Fifteenth Street and Main Street (the future Butler Avenue) in this 1920s photograph. A side wall along with a window and the rear piazza of one of Hotel Tybee's rental cottages can also be seen on the far right side of the photograph. This walkway was a shortcut to Tybee Island's downtown commercial district from Hotel Tybee's main entrance. (Courtesy of the Georgia Historical Society.)

HOTEL TYBEE

FIREPROOF

Savannah Beach, Georgia

American and European Plan

OPENING DINNER DANCE, MAY 28TH, 1932

Dinner Dance from 6:00 P. M. to 9:00 P. M.

Music by your favorite Doc Sauers and his full orchestra at $1.00 per person. No Cover charge

DANCING ON OCEAN PIER FROM 9:15 P. M. TO 12:00 P. M.
DOC SAUERS AND HIS FULL ORCHESTRA

There is no depression at Savannah Beach. Just new low rates to suit all. Come and meet your friends at the Informal Opening Dinner Dance at Hotel Tybee.

Reservations May Be Made by Telephone—No. 9102

Third Season Same Management

BEACH HOTEL OPERATING COMPANY

Newspapers were utilized to advertise hotels in order to generate business during Hotel Tybee's era. Shown above is a Hotel Tybee newspaper advertisement that appeared in the *Savannah Morning News* on May 26, 1932, announcing a dinner-dance to celebrate the opening of the busy 1932 summer season.

This photograph was taken in 1930 and shows young Hotel Tybee visitor John Conn and an unidentified young woman wading into the Atlantic Ocean from the beach directly in front of Hotel Tybee. (Courtesy of the Georgia Archives.)

54

Riding bicycles has always been a common form of transportation on Tybee Island. This woman is posing for a photograph while seated on her bicycle at rest on the concrete walkway between Hotel Tybee and Fifteenth Street. (Courtesy of Hank Buckley.)

These two women appear to be joking on the beach in front of Hotel Tybee in the 1920s. With numerous dancing pavilions, bars, and nightclubs located nearby, there was always fun to be had. (Courtesy of Hank Buckley.)

This special event (perhaps a footrace) was held on the beach in the 1920s between Hotel Tybee's beach pavilion and Tybrisa Pavilion. The photographer was located on Hotel Tybee's beach pavilion opposite Tybrisa Pavilion. (Courtesy of the Georgia Historical Society.)

This 1920s photograph of people of all ages walking, swimming, playing, and congregating on the beach near Tybrisa Pavilion was taken from Izlar's beach pavilion. The umbrella was a common form of sunscreen in those days. (Courtesy of the Georgia Historical Society.)

Orchestras were a very common form of musical entertainment during Hotel Tybee's era. Orchestras frequently performed at Hotel Tybee's dining room, bar, beach pavilion, meeting rooms, and beachside dance patio. This 1940s photograph shows a 10-piece orchestra beach parade that took place in front of Hotel Tybee. (Courtesy of the Georgia Historical Society.)

Six-, ten-, and twelve-piece orchestra concerts often took place on the beach, as seen in this 1940s photograph, which was taken just south of Tybrisa Pavilion. (Courtesy of the Georgia Historical Society.)

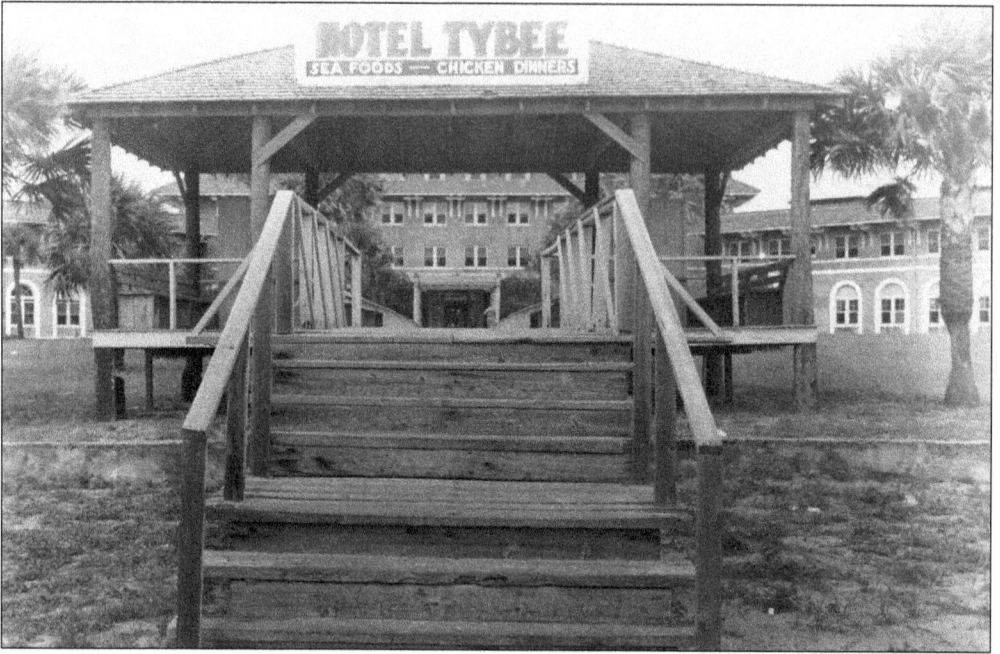

A sign above Hotel Tybee's stairway from the beach in this 1939 photograph advertises its restaurant's popular food offerings to the hundreds of beachgoers who pass by this point on the beach everyday. Generating such additional walk-in food-and-beverage revenue is instrumental in the quest of all full-service hotels to meet their budgeted revenue goals. (Courtesy of the Georgia Historical Society.)

This 1944 photograph, taken on Hotel Tybee's walkway to the beach, features, from left to right, Guy Witmer, Kay Witmer Davis, and Kate Shea. (Courtesy of Kitty Hernandez.)

The Cottonseed Crushers' Association of Georgia held its 1946 annual convention at Hotel Tybee. Its delegates are shown in the above photograph. This association frequently held its annual convention at Hotel Tybee. On May 10, 1925, the Atlantic Cotton Association, composed of leading cotton financiers, dealers, and authorities along the Eastern seaboard, also held its annual convention at Hotel Tybee. (Courtesy of the Georgia Historical Society.)

This 1947 photograph shows Eliza Bunny Faircloth (left) and Gloria Cravitz enjoying a beautiful summer day while sitting on the beachside patio at Hotel Tybee. Such fun summer days were filled with walking on the beach, playing in the surf, sunbathing, and making sand castles. (Courtesy of Kathy Layne.)

This 1941 photograph, taken from Main Street (the future Butler Avenue), shows most of the west-facing profile of Hotel Tybee. Hotel Tybee's train station, which had previously been located at this location, had been removed many years earlier since the last train from Tybee Island departed on

July 31, 1933. The demand for railroad transportation to and from Tybee Island tapered off after Tybee Road opened in 1923. (Courtesy of the Georgia Historical Society.)

This 1931 photograph, taken from Hotel Tybee's beachside courtyard, shows the east-facing profile of Hotel Tybee's main building. On July 22, 1931, a fire destroyed two city blocks, containing 20 wooden houses in Tybee Island's downtown commercial district, where Hotel Tybee was located. Hotel Tybee caught fire several times from sparks carried by the wind, and this caused a frenzy.

At one point, Hotel Tybee was just 100 yards from the fire's center. Firemen and soldiers from nearby Fort Screven kept the fire from causing any serious injury to the hotel or any of its guests. In one section of the fire zone where the water supply was limited, soft drinks were poured into tubs and thrown onto the blaze. (Courtesy of the Georgia Archives.)

Gloria Cravitz is seen sitting in a flower pot on the walkway to the beach in front of Hotel Tybee in 1947. Behind her can be seen cars parking at the beach's edge so that their drivers and passengers can enjoy a variety of amazing views, such as sunrises, moonrises, thunderstorms looming on the horizon, dolphins playing, and waves rolling in as well as men and women strolling by in the latest swimwear fashions. (Courtesy of Kathy Layne.)

Gloria Cravitz is seen posing on the concrete seawall and sidewalk in front of Hotel Tybee in 1957. This same spot was a popular surf-fishing spot at high tide because the ocean would submerge most of the seawall at high tide in those days. (Courtesy of Kathy Layne.)

The above image is a 1920s postcard of the west-facing profile and the well-landscaped entrance to Hotel Tybee. This postcard was one card of many contained in an old-fashioned postcard "accordion," which featured numerous colored postcards of Tybee Island and Savannah landmarks. (Courtesy of an anonymous donor.)

The above image is another 1920s postcard of the west-facing profile of and landscaped entrance to Hotel Tybee. Since the building of the first Hotel Tybee through the present day, postcards have always been very popular souvenir items as well as a way to communicate between friends and family. (Courtesy of an anonymous donor.)

HOTEL TYBEE, SAVANNAH BEACH, GEORGIA

This postcard shows Hotel Tybee's east-facing, beachside profile, as it would have appeared from the boardwalk to Hotel Tybee's beach pavilion in 1919. On May 30, 1919, a joint meeting of the Georgia Bar Association and South Carolina Bar Association of lawyers was held at Hotel Tybee. US attorney general A. Mitchell Palmer gave the keynote address, with the subject being "Germany's Commercial Invasion of America." (Courtesy of Florence Spirides.)

27—Hotel Tybee, Savannah Beach, Georgia

This 1920s postcard features a view of Hotel Tybee's west-facing profile from the air. On May 27, 1920, the Georgia Bar Association of lawyers again held its annual convention at Hotel Tybee. Prof. Roscoe Pound, dean of the Harvard University Law School, was the keynote speaker. (Courtesy of an anonymous donor.)

Station and Entrance, Tybee Hotel, Tybee Beach, near Savannah, Ga.

This postcard, which was sent in the US Mail on July 21, 1913, shows Hotel Tybee's main entrance along with its train station. Note the covered walkway extending from the hotel's main entry doors to the trackside platform to keep arriving-and-departing passengers dry during rainstorms and cool from direct sunlight on hot summer days. On July 16, 1926, the Southern Textile Association held its annual convention at Hotel Tybee. About 500 industry executives from Georgia, the Carolinas, and other Southern states rode the railroad to attend. The theme of the convention was the standardization of cotton textile products and processes. (Author's collection.)

This 1940s postcard, which captured a full moon–illuminated night, shows (on the right side of the image) the very popular Brass Rail restaurant and nightclub on the boardwalk with Hotel Tybee and a Ferris wheel directly behind it. A bingo parlor appears at the left side of the postcard. (Courtesy of Florence Spirides.)

Hotel Tybee and its beach pavilion and bathhouse clearly stand out just left of center on this 1920s postcard featuring a bird's-eye view of the eastern side of Tybee Island facing the Atlantic Ocean. To the left of Hotel Tybee's beach pavilion appears Izlar's beach pavilion and bathhouse, followed by Tybrisa Pavilion. Tybee Inlet borders on the left margin, and the Savannah River borders on the right margin. From the north end to the south end, Main Street (the future Butler Avenue) and the Central of Georgia Railway Company's tracks run down the center of the island. (Courtesy of the Tybee Island Historical Society.)

HAVING A BARREL OF FUN AT TYBEE

This humorous postcard was sold in Hotel Tybee's beach store as a souvenir of Tybee Island. Since the photograph features a barrel as well as what appears to be alcoholic beverage bottles, the postcard was probably sold during Prohibition. (Courtesy of John Duncan.)

In the late 1800s, a unique style of Tybee Island residential architecture emerged. The "raised cottage" was designed to withstand the often-harsh environmental conditions of low-lying coastal areas. Raised cottages, being elevated up in the air with wraparound porches and large windows and doors, allowed its tenants to thoroughly enjoy ocean breezes during Tybee Island's hot summer months since there was no air-conditioning available at the time. In the event of a passing hurricane, being in an elevated structure above a flooding tidal storm surge is a good thing for obvious reasons. The four-sided hipped roofs of raised cottages are very aerodynamic during windstorms and can withstand most winds blowing from any direction. The high pitch of these roofs also helped to cool interior rooms. Many raised cottages can be seen in this south-end aerial photograph, taken in 1932. The large Tybrisa Pavilion as well as Hotel Tybee's beach pavilion can be seen on the right side of this photograph. (Courtesy of Hank Buckley.)

This slightly overexposed late-1950s aerial photograph of Tybee Island's downtown commercial district shows Hotel Tybee on the far right side and Tybrisa Pavilion, pier, and bathhouse building toward the middle. (Courtesy of Clair Price.)

This 1937 aerial photograph shows the western side of Tybee Island, bordered by Tybee Inlet (also known today as the Back River). The western side of the island was mostly uninhabited at that time. Today, that same area is completely filled with mostly residential structures. The Atlantic Ocean appears in the distance, and the large Tybrisa Pavilion can be seen on the beach on the east side of the island. (Courtesy of the Georgia Historical Society.)

Hotel Tybee's west-facing profile appears in the center of this 1950s aerial photograph. As seen above, the five-acre Hotel Tybee tract of land encompassed an entire city block from Fourteenth Street to Fifteenth Street with 475 linear feet of prime beachfront real estate. A two-lane Butler Avenue with a grassy median appears along the bottom of the photograph. Today, Butler Avenue is a four-lane highway. In the upper right-hand corner of the photograph on Fifteenth Street appear the once very popular Brass Rail restaurant and nightclub and Hotel Tybee's rental cottages. (Courtesy of Florence Spirides.)

71

Hotel Tybee's east-facing, beachside profile appears in the center of this 1959 aerial photograph. Guest-room balconies made of concrete had just been built onto the hotel's north wing, which previously had none. Along the right side of the photograph is Fourteenth Street with Ocean Terrace Motel and Mrs. Taylor's Restaurant being located oceanfront at Fourteenth Street. Hotel Tybee's rental cottages and Nickie's Bar are located along the left side of the photograph on Fifteenth Street. (Courtesy of Barbara Wright.)

This newspaper advertisement ran in the June 11, 1942, edition of the *Augusta Chronicle*. Tybee Island's beach is the closest beach to Augusta, Georgia, and Hotel Tybee frequently advertised in that market to encourage Augusta residents to spend their vacations and convene group meetings at Hotel Tybee. (Author's collection.)

Vacations Begin at

HOTEL TYBEE

SAVANNAH BEACH

Georgia's Playground

Frequent bus and train schedules make gas and oil unnecessary.

Special vacation rates including double rooms with bath—all meals and amusements—$25.00 week, per person.

Regular room rates begin at $2.00 daily single and $3.00 daily double.

You will enjoy vacationing at Hotel Tybee now before heavy summer travel starts.

Write or wire for reservations to

HOTEL TYBEE
ON THE OCEAN ·
SAVANNAH BEACH, GEORGIA

In the 1950s, this Hotel Tybee newspaper advertisement ran in several newspapers throughout the region, such as in the metropolitan areas of Atlanta, Macon, and Augusta, Georgia; Chattanooga and Knoxville, Tennessee; Charlotte, North Carolina; Jacksonville, Florida; and Columbia, South Carolina. (Courtesy of the Georgia Historical Society.)

FOR A PLEASANT VACATION ON THE ATLANTIC COAST

VISIT

THE HOTEL TYBEE — SAVANNAH BEACH, GEORGIA

On the Ocean front, with miles of beautiful beach. A modern resort hotel, featuring every comfort and convenience of the metropolitan areas. An ideal place for conventions, conferences or group meetings, banquets and parties. Popular bands play nightly for your dancing pleasure in our PATIO UNDER THE STARS.

RATES UPON REQUEST

Furnished Cottages   Honeymoon Tower Suites

This 1950 photograph was taken during the Retail Credit Corporation's annual convention, which was held that year at Hotel Tybee. Also during 1950, the Georgia Chapter of the National Association of Postmasters held its annual convention at Hotel Tybee. About 400 postmasters attended. Jesse M. Donaldson, postmaster general of the United States, attended as a speaker. (Courtesy of Mary Frances Robertson.)

Jon and Nancy Byrd ate cake at their wedding reception, which was held in Hotel Tybee's main dining room in 1959. Weddings were a common occurrence at Hotel Tybee throughout the seven decades of its existence. (Courtesy of Nancy Byrd.)

Jon and Nancy Byrd were pelted with rice when they departed their wedding reception through the front doors of Hotel Tybee in 1959. Nancy had worked for Hotel Tybee general manager George L. Spirides at his ice-cream shop on the Tybee Island boardwalk when she was 14 years old. (Courtesy of Nancy Byrd.)

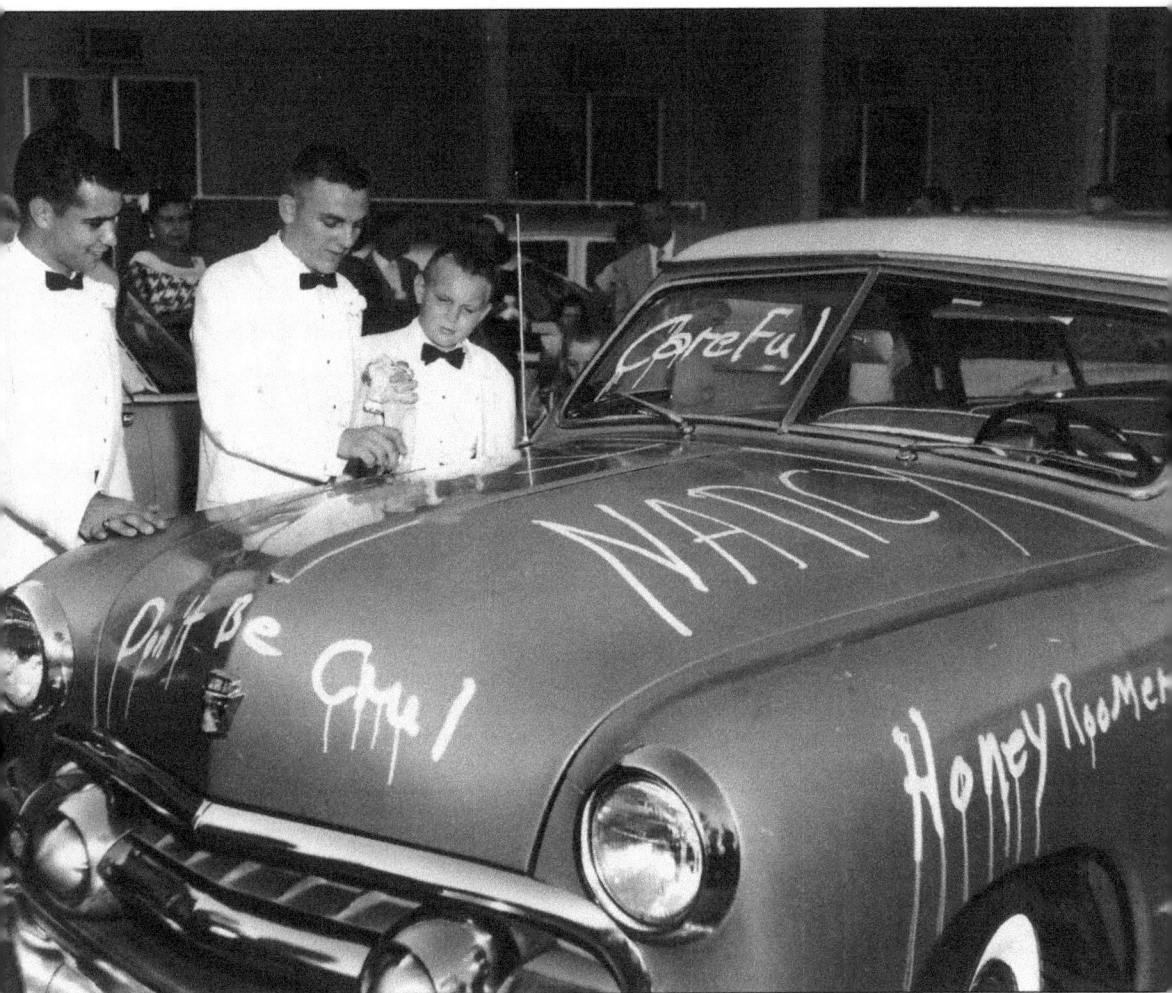

Jon and Nancy Byrd's car was thoroughly decorated outside of Hotel Tybee during their wedding reception in 1959. (Courtesy of Nancy Byrd.)

This photograph of Hotel Tybee's east-facing, beachside profile was taken from the southeast corner of the Hotel Tybee parcel of land in 1957 near the intersection of Fifteenth Street and the Strand. (Courtesy of the Georgia Archives.)

This 1959 postcard of Hotel Tybee's west-facing profile features a pretty lady in a swimsuit standing next to an oleander bush at the hotel's Butler Avenue entrance. Palm trees and oleanders were heavily used for landscaping at Hotel Tybee over the decades. Both of these plants are drought resistant as well as wind resistant and thrive in the soil conditions found on Tybee Island. (Courtesy of Florence Spirides.)

George Leonidas Spirides was the last Hotel Tybee general manager. He appears in this 1956 photograph taken in front of the main entrance doors to Hotel Tybee. George Leonidas Spirides (1896–1992) immigrated to the United States from Sparta, Greece, in 1910 at the age of 14. He spent the next five years working in New York City as a dishwasher, cook, and flower delivery boy. In 1915, George Spirides moved to Endicott, New York, to work serving food and beverages for his first cousin James Strates, owner of Strates Shows, which became the nation's largest traveling carnival show. Throughout the 1930s, George Spirides owned florist shops across New York State. In 1940, he married his wife, Florence, in Elmira, New York, and moved to Savannah, Georgia. For the next five years, George owned and/or managed restaurants in Savannah. In 1945, George and Florence Spirides moved to Tybee Island. They opened their first Tybee Island business in 1945, an ice-cream shop known as Frozen Delight, located on the boardwalk directly in front of Tybrisa Pavilion, one block south of Hotel Tybee. He later leased and managed Tybrisa Pavilion before becoming general manager of Hotel Tybee. (Courtesy of Florence Spirides.)

Hotel Tybee general manager George L. Spirides (left) appears with Hotel Tybee food-and-beverage manager Pete Manos in this 1957 photograph, which was taken outside a Hotel Tybee rental cottage on Fifteenth Street. Hotel Tybee prided itself on its high-quality culinary offerings. The menu was extensive and varied and usually offered fresh seafood and other items of American cuisine at moderate prices. The wait staff always paid particular attention to the needs of its guests. The main dining room seated 300 people and served breakfast, lunch, and dinner. Catering to large and small groups of people, as well as individual guests, was the specialty of Hotel Tybee's highly trained food-and-beverage staff. Hotel Tybee's kitchen featured the most modern of cooking appliances, and its ice-making machines produced 15 tons of ice daily. (Courtesy of Florence Spirides.)

In 1957, George Leonidas Spirides was joined by his nephew George Harry Spirides (1932–1995), the father of this book's author. George Harry Spirides had traveled from Sparta, Greece, to work for his uncle George at Hotel Tybee as a hotel maintenance man and groundskeeper while studying electrical engineering at Armstrong State College in Savannah. George Harry Spirides traveled from Greece by ship, arriving in New York City where he was welcomed to America by his Uncle George and Aunt Florence. This 1958 photograph shows George Harry Spirides standing in front of Hotel Tybee's south wing. (Courtesy of Florence Spirides.)

DONALD R. LIVINGSTON
POST OFFICE BOX 242
SAVANNAH, GEORGIA
June 16, 1958

Mr. George L. Spirides
Savannah Beach, Georgia

Dear Mr. Spirides:

This will acknowledge notice of employment of
your nephew, George H. Spirides, as maintenance man and
yard man during the summer season at the Tybee Hotel for
$15.00 per week; this letter approves such action.

Very truly yours

SEAVIEW DEVELOPMENT COMPANY

BY *Donald R. Livingston*
Donald R. Livingston
President

DRL/fe

This letter was written by Hotel Tybee owner Donald Livingston in 1958 to acknowledge that George Harry Spirides was employed at Hotel Tybee as a maintenance man and groundskeeper. George Harry Spirides reported to his Uncle George Leonidas Spirides, who was Hotel Tybee's general manager. Through his hard work, extreme determination, and dedication, George Harry Spirides worked up through the ranks over the years in every conceivable job in the hotel business and eventually acquired most of the Hotel Tybee tract of land where he built today's Ocean Plaza Beach Resort. (Courtesy of Florence Spirides.)

Hotel Tybee possessed five acres of landscaped green space that had to be regularly maintained. This 1959 photograph shows George Harry Spirides, Hotel Tybee maintenance man and groundskeeper, mowing grass at Hotel Tybee, as acknowledged in the letter shown on the opposite page. (Courtesy of Florence Spirides.)

Florence Spirides, wife of Hotel Tybee general manager George Leonidas Spirides, appears standing in the beachside courtyard of Hotel Tybee in this 1956 photograph. Florence was not only the love of George's life but also his business assistant and confidant in all his endeavors. (Courtesy of Florence Spirides.)

This 1959 postcard shows Ocean Terrace Motel, which was built on a Hotel Tybee vacant outparcel of oceanfront land at Fourteenth Street and the Strand at the northeast corner of the Hotel Tybee tract of land. It later became known as the Sands Motel. Between 1964 and 1966, George Harry Spirides leased and operated the Ocean Terrace Motel for his own account. (Courtesy of Florence Spirides.)

Three

HOTEL TYBEE'S
SUCCESSOR BUSINESSES

1961 TO PRESENT

On February 1, 1961, most of Hotel Tybee was demolished by Monroe Wrecking Company of Savannah. This 1965 postcard shows the Tybee Motel, which was the last remaining section (the north wing) of the once majestic Hotel Tybee after its main building and south wing were demolished by its owners at the time, the Seaview Development Company. (Courtesy of Frances Spirides.)

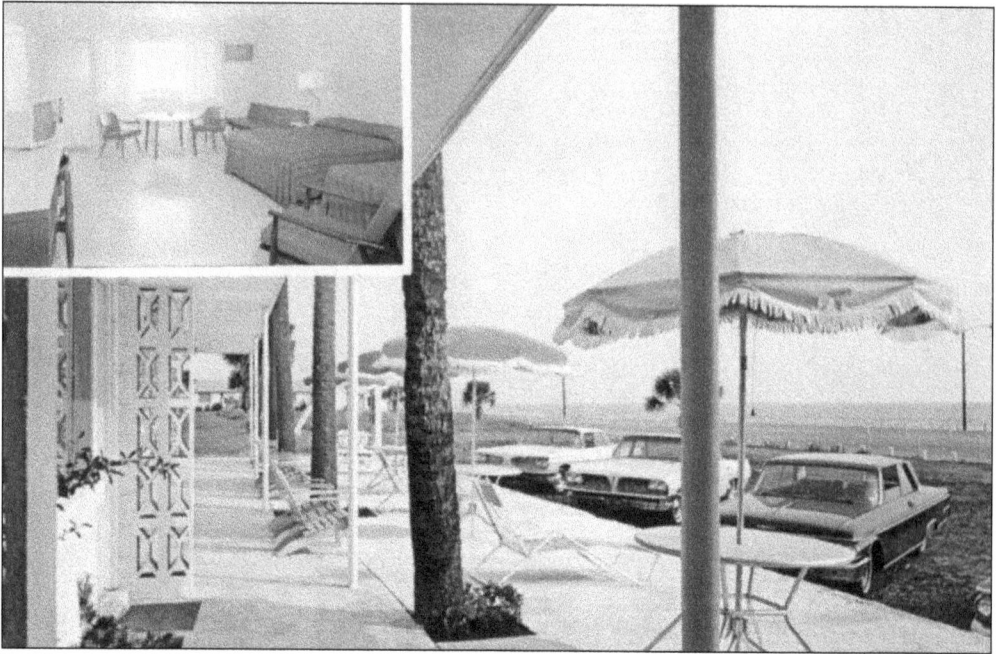

During the 1961–1964 period of time after Hotel Tybee had been torn down by its owners, George Harry Spirides attended college and worked at the newly constructed Ocean Plaza Motel. The original Ocean Plaza Motel, as seen above, was a one-story motel consisting of 25 guest rooms that had been built by George Leonidas Spirides in 1963 on a piece of oceanfront land at Fifteenth Street and the Strand at the southeast corner of the former Hotel Tybee tract of land. (Courtesy of Florence Spirides.)

This 1964 photograph shows George Leonidas Spirides proudly standing behind the front desk at Ocean Plaza Motel, which he owned and operated. This front desk became famous in the 1976 action movie Gator, starring Burt Reynolds and Jerry Reed. In that movie, Savannah mayor John Rousakis played the desk clerk who checked in Burt Reynolds at that same front desk before the bad guys blew up part of the Ocean Plaza Motel. (Courtesy of Florence Spirides.)

In September 1966, when this photograph was taken, George Harry Spirides married his wife, Frances, who was originally from Knoxville, Tennessee. Working closely most of the time with her husband, Frances ultimately worked for 43 years overseeing front desk, housekeeping, and accounting operations in the Spirides family's hotel business, located on the former Hotel Tybee tract of land, until she retired in 2009. (Courtesy of Frances Spirides.)

On March 1, 1967, Veranda Motel, Inc., with George Harry Spirides being one of its stockholders, purchased the last remaining section of Hotel Tybee (its north wing) with its attached real estate and renamed it Veranda Motel. This postcard, which was produced in the early 1970s, shows the first phase of the 45-room Veranda Motel, which was built by George Harry Spirides and partners on the northeast oceanfront portion of former Hotel Tybee's land. It backed up to the Ocean Terrace Motel, which had been built at Fourteenth Street and the Strand. The last remaining section of Hotel Tybee (its north wing) can be seen on the left side of the photograph. (Courtesy of Frances Spirides.)

In 1969, the very first Days Inn in the world was built by Cecil B. Day, founder of the Days Inn motel chain, on the former Hotel Tybee's northwestern parcel of land, located on Butler Avenue at Fourteenth Street. Cecil Day had lived for many years on Fourteenth Street near the site of his future motel. He asked his friend George Harry Spirides to assist him in building and managing his new motel, which was located directly adjacent to George H. Spirides's Veranda Motel. George Spirides agreed, and he became the first manager of the world's first Days Inn. (Courtesy of Frances Spirides.)

This early-1980s postcard shows the Veranda Motel, an expanded, two-story structure with 65 guest rooms, and the Veranda Restaurant, which had been built and operated by George H. Spirides on the northeast oceanfront portion of the former Hotel Tybee parcel of land. (Courtesy of Frances Spirides.)

This 1980s photograph shows the front of the Veranda Restaurant, which was built by George H. Spirides on the center-eastern portion of the former Hotel Tybee tract of land. This 100-seat restaurant overlooked the beach and served breakfast, lunch, and dinner. The children of George and Frances Spirides, Jeannie and Harry (the author of this book), worked every job in the Veranda Restaurant and at the Veranda Motel during all of their teenage years and into their twenties. (Courtesy of Frances Spirides.)

In addition to being a convenient dining spot for guests of Veranda Motel, the Veranda Restaurant was very popular for hungry beachgoers wanting hamburgers, French fries, corn dogs, milk shakes, and pizzas while they enjoyed their day at the beach. This photograph shows the interior of the Veranda Restaurant in the late 1980s. (Courtesy of Frances Spirides.)

Here the George H. Spirides family is photographed while standing behind the front desk at the grand opening of their new Ocean Plaza Beach Resort in March 1989 when its south hotel building opened for business. Members of the Spirides family shown are, from left to right, George H., Jeannie, Frances, and Harry Spirides (the author of this book). This new Ocean Plaza was built and operated by George Harry Spirides until his death in 1995. Harry Spirides assumed control of the Spirides family hotel business upon his father's death. The south hotel building, as with the north hotel building, is built of concrete, features 102 hotel guest rooms, and has fire sprinklers and elevators. (Courtesy of Frances Spirides.)

Ocean Plaza Beach Resort's north hotel building, shown on the right side of this photograph, was built four years later in 1993 and added another 102 hotel guest rooms to its inventory, thus bringing Ocean Plaza's total hotel guest room count to 204. This photograph shows both the south hotel building and the north hotel building joined together by the Dolphin Reef Oceanfront Restaurant & Lounge. Ocean Plaza's beach frontage of 475 linear feet is the same amount and in the same spot as Hotel Tybee's guests enjoyed decades earlier. (Author's collection.)

The above photograph shows a double queen sized–bed guest room type at Ocean Plaza Beach Resort. With the large numbers of traveling families and other groups (more than 100,000 people visit Ocean Plaza each year), this type of room configuration is the most popular. Unlike Hotel Tybee, all of Ocean Plaza's guest rooms have private balconies. Ocean Plaza's hotel guest rooms are located 200 feet closer to the Atlantic Ocean than those of the second Hotel Tybee. Perhaps this is because the land is four feet higher in elevation in the spot where the second Hotel Tybee was built, and in case of a hurricane tidal storm surge, that spot might have been a little safer. (Author's collection.)

Three generations of Tybee Island hoteliers who have worked at the Hotel Tybee property appear in this Christmas 1989 photograph. Seated are, from left to right, George Leonidas Spirides, George Harry Spirides, and Harry Leonidas Spirides, the father of George Harry Spirides who worked for many years along with his wife, Eugenia, assisting their son in his hotel business. Standing is Harry George Spirides (the author of this book). Perhaps, Harry G. Spirides's young daughters Katie and Ava will follow in his footsteps and become fourth-generation hoteliers. (Courtesy of Frances Spirides.)

George H. Spirides's final dream was to build an upscale oceanfront restaurant at Ocean Plaza. His son Harry fulfilled his dream when Harry built and opened the Dolphin Reef Oceanfront Restaurant & Lounge. Seen here addressing a crowd at the grand opening of his Dolphin Reef Oceanfront Restaurant & Lounge in April 2000 is the author of this book and chief executive officer of Ocean Plaza Beach Resort, Harry G. Spirides. (Courtesy of Frances Spirides.)

Dolphin Reef Oceanfront Restaurant & Lounge can be seen in the upper center of the above photograph, located between Ocean Plaza Beach Resort's south and north hotel buildings. With seating for 300 people and spectacular ocean views, Dolphin Reef rivals Hotel Tybee's dining facilities and culinary offerings that once existed on the same property some 50 to 100 years earlier. (Author's collection.)

Dolphin Reef Oceanfront Restaurant & Lounge sports a trendy and fun underwater dolphin theme throughout its facility. At right is a photograph of its entrance, which is decorated with replicas of seaweed, dolphins, waves, and bubbles. With its in-house food-and-beverage department, Ocean Plaza Beach Resort is the only full-service hotel on Tybee Island. Dolphin Reef is open for breakfast, lunch, dinner, hotel room service, and banquet catering year-round. (Author's collection.)

Through its windows, which are 37 feet tall, Dolphin Reef Oceanfront Restaurant & Lounge features breathtaking views of the Atlantic Ocean, nearby beaches, and the Tybee Island ocean pier and pavilion. Additionally, Dolphin Reef is the preferred spot to host a wedding reception or watch the sunrise, moonrise, ships transiting into and out of the Port of Savannah, and fireworks displays, which are launched from the nearby ocean pier during special events like New Year's Eve, Independence Day, and Labor Day. (Author's collection.)

With Dolphin Reef's large hand-painted murals of sea life; a bar countertop made of terrazzo tile, supported by glass blocks with bubbles in them; metal stairway railings that look like seaweed; wooden millwork on the walls with bubbles cut into it; a wavy ceiling; and various hues of blue and green used throughout, the bar gives visitors a feeling of being underwater. (Author's collection.)

Ocean Plaza Beach Resort's conference center is the last remaining section of Hotel Tybee. That building was once Hotel Tybee's north wing and housed its main dining room on the ground floor with hotel rooms on the second floor. Today, that building is more than 101 years old and is still in good condition due to renovations and a good maintenance program by Ocean Plaza's engineering staff. (Author's collection.)

Tybee Island remains one of Georgia's favorite beach-destination wedding venues, and Ocean Plaza's full-service conference center is the perfect place to host all types of banquets and receptions. Its banquet menus offer a wide range of items to match any taste or budget. As was the case 100 years ago when that building was a part of Hotel Tybee, wedding receptions are still frequently held there. (Author's collection.)

As was the case with this same space 100 years ago when it was Hotel Tybee's main dining room, companies, government agencies, associations, and other organizations still enjoy hosting training seminars, meetings, and lectures in Ocean Plaza's conference center. Garden Rooms Nos. 1 and 2 are shown in this photograph set up in a classroom-style configuration. (Author's collection.)

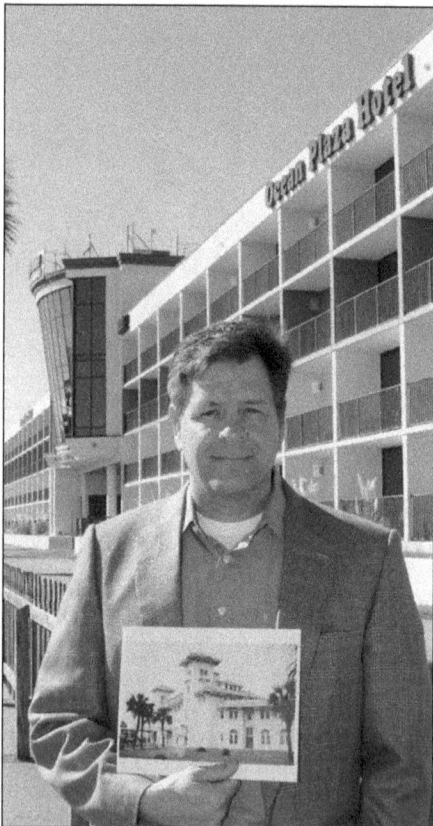

Author Harry G. Spirides is shown in this photograph holding an image of Hotel Tybee while standing in front of his family's Ocean Plaza Beach Resort, which is built at the same address where Hotel Tybee once stood. Harry Spirides is very passionate about preserving the rich history and long tradition of accommodating visitors and serving hospitality at this property. His dream is to one day lead a renovation and expansion of his family's resort property to make it look similar to the second Hotel Tybee with its majestic Spanish Revival architecture. One important component of this proposed expansion is a new modern convention center. Such a facility would attract groups of people to Tybee Island during the slower, "off-season" months that encompass the majority of the year. Harry Spirides graduated from Benedictine Military High School of Savannah. He holds a bachelor of science degree in hospitality administration from Florida State University and a master of business administration degree from Mercer University. A military veteran, Harry Spirides proudly served this country as a US Coast Guard officer. He served three years active duty and eight years reserve duty. He separated from the service with an honorable discharge in 2008. (Author's collection.)

Above is a conceptual drawing of the entry driveway of author Harry Spirides's proposed future redevelopment and expansion of Ocean Plaza Beach Resort. Through his proposed redevelopment project, Harry's goal is to make the resort property look similar to the second Hotel Tybee with its majestic Spanish Revival style of architecture and add a modern convention center with 30,000 square feet of meeting space, more hotel guest rooms, retail shops, a tropical resort-type swimming pool, a fitness center, and a multilevel parking garage—all of which he says the Tybee Island downtown commercial district greatly needs in order to accommodate existing demand, level out the extreme seasonal nature of the island's economy, and to remain competitive with other resort destinations. (Courtesy of CMMI Architects.)

The existing Ocean Plaza south hotel building, north hotel building, and Dolphin Reef Restaurant & Lounge will all be renovated and incorporated into the Ocean Plaza redevelopment project. Harry Spirides is currently in the process of seeking sources of financing to fund his "Hotel Tybee No. 3" project. This conceptual drawing shows the proposed future east-facing, beachside profile after the Ocean Plaza Beach Resort Hotel Tybee redevelopment project is completed. (Courtesy of CMMI Architects.)

Four

TYBRISA PAVILION
1901–1967

Tybrisa Pavilion was located on the beach adjacent to Hotel Tybee. As seen on the right side of this 1930s photograph, Tybrisa Pavilion was a 21,000-square-foot, ocean-side, multipurpose, covered structure that was a wonderful amenity for Hotel Tybee guests to enjoy. Tybrisa Pavilion was built in March 1901 by the Central of Georgia Railway Company to encourage people to ride its trains for a fun-filled visit to destination Tybee Island. It was one of the Savannah area's most popular recreational spots. Tybrisa Bathhouse building can be seen in the left side of this photograph. (Courtesy of the Georgia Historical Society.)

This photograph shows the south-facing profile of the all–wooden frame Tybrisa Pavilion in the early 1900s. The Tybrisa Pavilion and Bathhouse complex was regarded by most people as being at the heart of the tourism and hospitality industry on Tybee Island. (Courtesy of the Tybee Island Historical Society.)

With the flat, well-compacted sand on Tybee Island's beaches, it was often commonplace to see Army soldiers from Fort Screven, which was located on the north end of Tybee Island, march in formation during special events at Tybrisa Pavilion, as seen in this 1924 photograph. (Courtesy of the Georgia Historical Society.)

This 1924 photograph shows a special event being held at Tybrisa Pavilion. On the left side of the photograph is the pavilion, with the bathhouse and picnic pavilion being located on the right side. In 1925, Tybrisa's bathhouse was equipped with 525 bathrooms for changing and showering. (Courtesy of the Georgia Historical Society.)

In 1925, the top floor of the Tybrisa Bathhouse building was enclosed with windows, located between the columns, along with wood siding. This created two large auditoriums on the top floor, which were used for large gatherings. This mid-1920s photograph shows the Tybrisa Bathhouse building along with its 50,000-gallon water tank on Sixteenth Street (today called Tybrisa Street). (Courtesy of the Georgia Historical Society.)

Among many other uses, Tybrisa Pavilion was used as a classroom to present lectures and administer tests. (Courtesy of the Georgia Historical Society.)

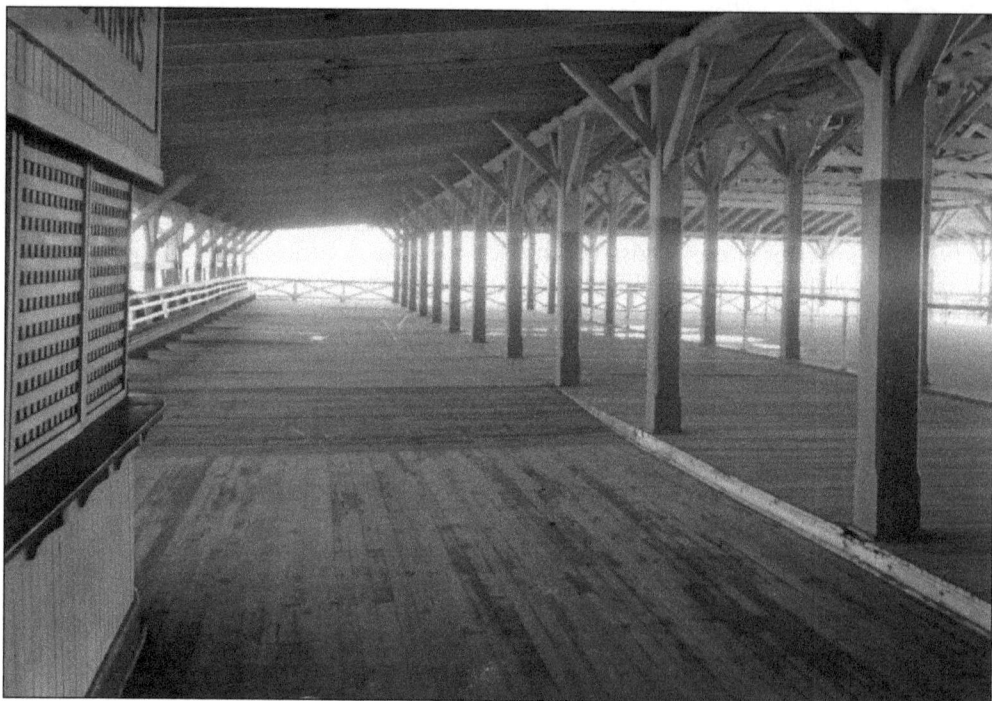

This photograph was shot while looking east through Tybrisa Pavilion toward the Atlantic Ocean. Tybrisa Pavilion was a great place to catch fish, meet new friends, and enjoy fresh sea breezes and pristine views of the Atlantic Ocean. (Courtesy of the Georgia Historical Society.)

Over its 66 years of existence, Tybrisa Pavilion hosted hundreds of dances and other social events. In both of these photographs, an elevated stage can be seen where musicians performed. Roller-skating was also another popular activity held at Tybrisa Pavilion. Coin-operated rides were also offered there for the entertainment of children. (Both, courtesy of the Georgia Historical Society.)

Tybrisa Pavilion's very profitable food-and-beverage concession stands can be seen in this photograph. Hot dogs, hamburgers, ice cream, French fries, coffee, and soft drinks could all be purchased at the Tybrisa Pavilion. (Courtesy of the Georgia Historical Society.)

George Leonidas Spirides and his wife, Florence, moved to Tybee Island from Savannah in 1945. That same year, they opened their ice-cream shop called Frozen Delight on the Tybee Island boardwalk at Tybrisa Pavilion. This 1945 photograph shows the Spirides family's ice-cream shop on the left. (Courtesy of Florence Spirides.)

This 1947 photograph, while looking north, shows a crowded Tybee Island boardwalk between Tybrisa Pavilion and its bathhouse building, which contained a restaurant, bar, and bowling alley. The Spirides family's ice-cream shop can be seen on the left. Brass Rail restaurant and nightclub along with a Ferris wheel can be seen in the distance. (Courtesy of Florence Spirides.)

While looking north in this 1947 photograph, which was taken from Tybrisa Pavilion, one can see the Tybee Island boardwalk along with a bingo parlor just left of center, Brass Rail restaurant and nightclub, with a Ferris wheel behind it, is just right of center, and the concrete seawall and Atlantic Ocean are on the right. (Courtesy of Florence Spirides.)

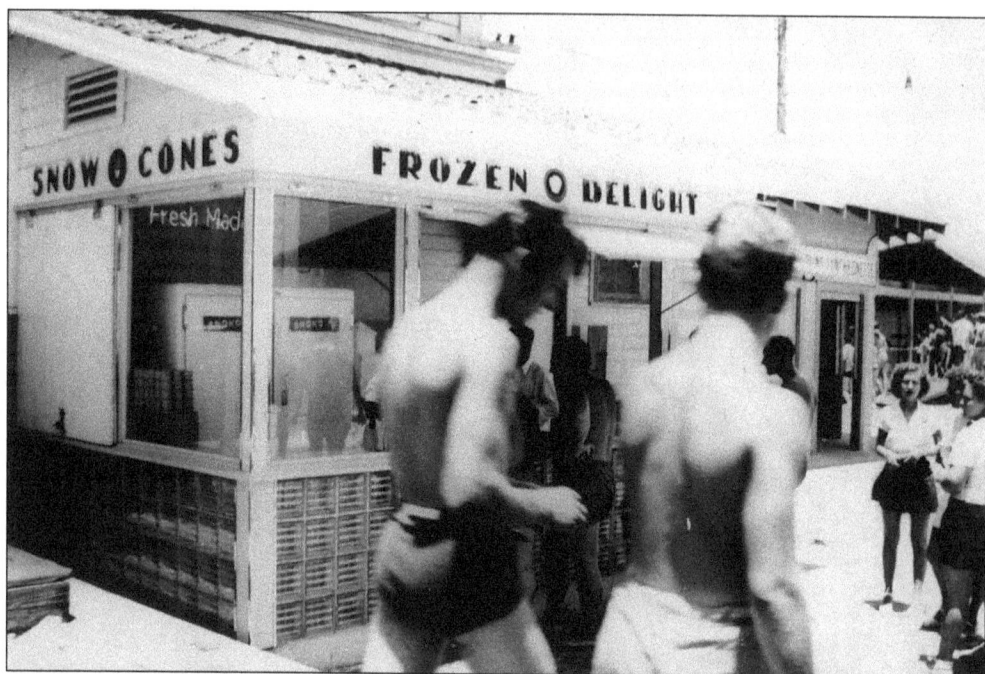

The Spirides family's Frozen Delight ice-cream shop on the Tybee Island boardwalk at Tybrisa Pavilion in 1945 was a very popular place to buy ice cream, frozen custard, and snow cones as well as meet new friends. (Courtesy Florence Spirides.)

George L. Spirides can be seen working alongside two of his employees at his Frozen Delight ice-cream shop in this 1947 photograph. (Courtesy of Florence Spirides.)

George L. Spirides (right) can be seen in this 1945 photograph speaking with business associate Earl Truax outside of the Spirides family's ice-cream shop on the Tybee Island boardwalk at Tybrisa Pavilion. (Courtesy of Florence Spirides.)

Since the earliest days of Tybrisa Pavilion, photograph concession stands were very commonplace. Here, a family poses for a Tybee souvenir photograph in the early 1900s. (Courtesy of Paula Branson.)

The hurricane of October 15, 1947, did extensive damage to Tybrisa Pavilion and related buildings. (Hurricanes were not named back then.) This photograph was taken during that storm. It was a Category 1 on the Saffir-Simpson Hurricane Scale and made landfall 15 miles south of Savannah, Georgia, producing winds of 85 miles per hour, a four-foot-tall storm surge, and one known fatality. (Courtesy of Florence Spirides.)

Before striking the Savannah area, the same hurricane hit the Miami, Florida, area where it produced 15 inches of rain and catastrophic flooding. The above photograph shows the Tybrisa Pavilion being damaged by that hurricane. (Courtesy of Florence Spirides.)

In this photograph, the damage to the Tybrisa Bathhouse building by the hurricane of October 15, 1947, can be seen. Crashing waves smashed the front stairways as well as most of the front wall. The Spirides family's ice-cream shop also sustained a lot of damage. (Courtesy of Florence Spirides.)

In early 1949, after the 1947 hurricane had seriously damaged Tybrisa Pavilion, George L. Spirides leased that structure for five years from its owner, the Tybrisa Corporation, whose main shareholder was William Haar. Mr. Haar had no intention of repairing the Tybrisa Pavilion at that time. During the spring of 1949, George L. Spirides repaired and completely restored that landmark attraction, and it once again became an entertainment complex for adults and kids alike. (Courtesy of Florence Spirides.)

Fifty wood pilings underneath Tybrisa Pavilion were washed away by the 1947 hurricane. Many steps were destroyed, much of the flooring was torn up, and a large part of the roof was wrecked. This 1949 photograph shows George L. Spirides (left) with an unidentified assistant making repairs to Tybrisa Pavilion. (Courtesy of Florence Spirides.)

In the 1950s, a fishing pier was built onto the eastern end of Tybrisa Pavilion, which gave its visitors the option to try their luck at fishing even at low tide. This 1950s photograph, taken from Fourteenth Street and the Strand in front of Hotel Tybee, shows the fishing pier extending from the eastern end of Tybrisa Pavilion. On the right side of the photograph in the distance, the Brass Rail restaurant and nightclub can be seen. (Author's collection.)

This 1961 photograph, which was taken from the Tybrisa fishing pier, shows the east end of Tybrisa Pavilion. One of the most popular places to relax on Tybee Island at low tide during a hot summer day was on the beach underneath the Tybrisa Pavilion. (Courtesy of the Georgia Historical Society.)

Hotel Tybee can be seen behind Brass Rail restaurant and nightclub on the far right side of this 1950s photograph, which was taken on the Tybrisa fishing pier. (Courtesy of an anonymous donor.)

This 1960s photograph shows the south-facing profile of Tybrisa Pavilion. Many sections of the pavilion had been enclosed over the years to provide secure spaces to sell concessions. (Courtesy of the Tybee Island Historical Society.)

This photograph of the south-facing profile of Tybrisa Pavilion was taken at Sixteenth Street (later renamed Tybrisa Street) shortly before it and its adjoining bathhouse, restaurant, and bowling alley building burned down to the ground in a fire that ravaged a full city block on May 16, 1967. Smoke from the blaze could be seen in Savannah, 20 miles away. (Courtesy of Florence Spirides.)

This early-1920s photograph shows people enjoying the beach and surf near Hotel Tybee. Two men wearing hats can be seen in the foreground sitting on the railing at the southeast corner of Hotel Tybee's dancing and special event beach pavilion. Also in the foreground, note the Hotel Tybee lifeboat with life ring at the ready. In the distance can be seen Tybrisa Pavilion. (Courtesy of Florence Spirides.)

This 1950s photograph shows the long-standing and very popular Brass Rail restaurant and nightclub, which was located on Fifteenth Street at The Strand adjacent to Hotel Tybee and Tybrisa Pavilion. It featured an orchestra pit suspended over its dance floor. Countless Hotel Tybee guests spent many nights in this William Haar–owned establishment. (Courtesy of Florence Spirides.)

George Leonidas Spirides and his wife, Florence, can be seen in this 1971 photograph, which was taken during the demolition of Brass Rail restaurant and nightclub. The City of Tybee Island/ Savannah Beach had purchased that land and buildings to enlarge its adjacent Strand municipal parking lot. (Courtesy of Florence Spirides.)

Five

SAVANNAH-TO-TYBEE
RAILROAD
1887–1933

Above is a 1914 photograph of the Central of Georgia Railway Company's locomotive Engine No. 1537 with its attached passenger cars and an unidentified crew at Tybee Island. The train station's "platform" here is made of gravel. This quick and convenient railroad transportation link, which was built in 1886–1887, was absolutely instrumental in making Hotel Tybee into the very popular beach resort destination that it ultimately became. (Courtesy of Ed Mims.)

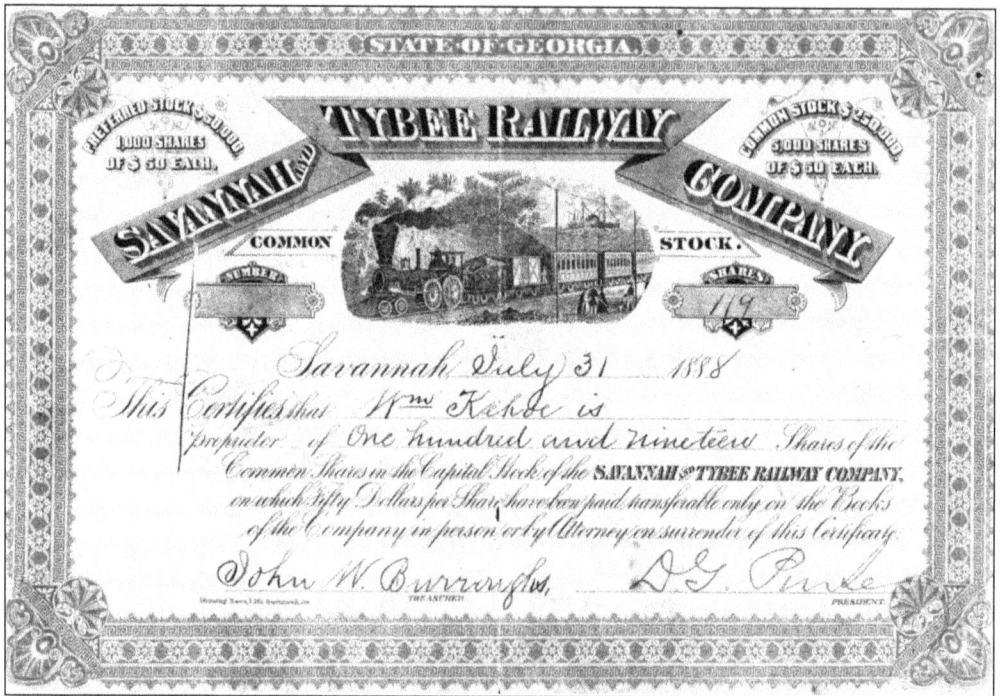

The Savannah & Tybee Railway Company was incorporated in November 1885 under a charter granted by the Georgia General Assembly. Above is a copy of one of the original stock certificates issued by that company. It was issued to William Kehoe and signed by John Burroughs and Daniel Purse on July 31, 1888. The Central of Georgia Railway Company later acquired this company and named this section of railroad track its Tybee Branch. (Courtesy of the Central of Georgia Railway Historical Society.)

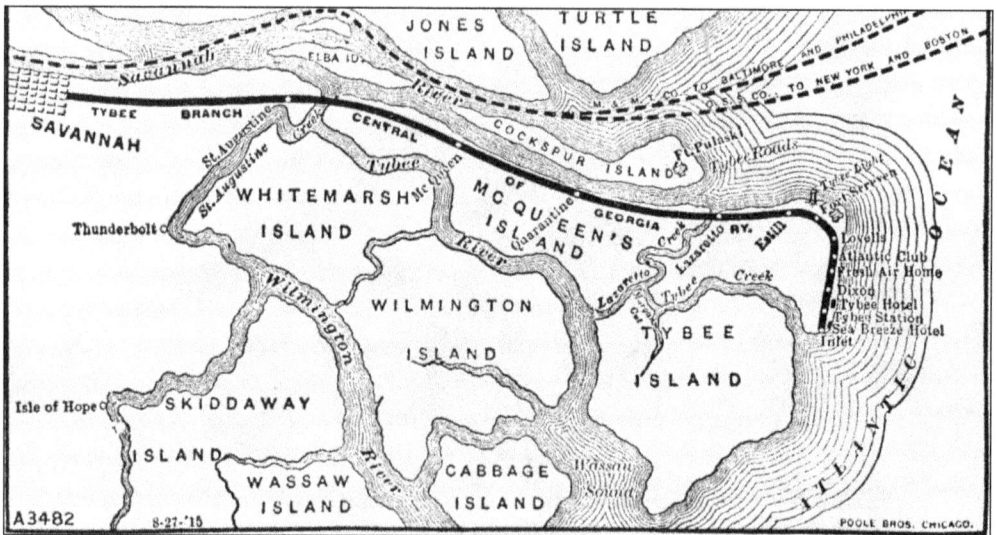

The general route of the 17.7-mile-long railway line between Savannah and Tybee Island is shown on this 1915 Central of Georgia Railway Company map, which lists 12 stops. Both St. Augustine Creek and Lazaretto Creek are large navigable waterways over which bridges were built. (Courtesy of the Central of Georgia Railway Historical Society.)

Above is a photograph of the Central of Georgia Railway Company's Tybee Island train depot, which was located in Savannah on Randolph Street at Presidents Street. The first train to Tybee Island made the run on July 18, 1887. (Courtesy of the Georgia Historical Society.)

Prior to Capt. Daniel G. Purse building his railroad, travelers had to make a two-hour trip by steamboat from Savannah to Tybee Island. Government and business officials of the time understood that Tybee Island could never attain the popularity it promised as a resort destination until the transit time between Savannah and Tybee Island was reduced to the absolute minimum. Shown here is a copy of a Central of Georgia Railway Company train schedule that shows the number of passenger trains that operated daily between Savannah and Tybee Island during the summer of 1913. (Courtesy of the Georgia Historical Society.)

SCHEDULES
BETWEEN SAVANNAH AND
TYBEE
Where Ocean Breezes Blow

TAKING EFFECT JUNE 21, 1913

Central (90th Meridian) Time, one hour slower than Savannah City Time

WEEK DAYS		SUNDAYS	
LEAVE SAVANNAH	LEAVE TYBEE	LEAVE SAVANNAH	LEAVE TYBEE
6.00 AM	6.00 AM	7.10 AM	7.00 AM
9.00 AM	7.00 AM	9.00 AM	8.00 AM
10.25 AM	10.00 AM	10.00 AM	10.15 AM
12.01 PM	11.15 AM	11.00 AM	11.15 AM
2.30 PM	1.30 PM	12.01 PM	12.15 PM
3.00 PM	4.05 PM	*1.45 PM	1.00 PM
4.15 PM	5.05 PM	*2.15 PM	3.30 PM
5.15 PM	6.05 PM	2.30 PM	*4.30 PM
6.15 PM	7.05 PM	3.35 PM	*5.00 PM
7.15 PM	8.10 PM	*4.30 PM	*5.30 PM
*9.20 PM	9.10 PM	5.00 PM	*6.05 PM
ADDITIONAL TRAINS TUESDAYS AND THURSDAYS		6.30 PM	7.00 PM
		7.10 PM	8.00 PM
5.20 PM	11.00 PM	9.00 PM	9.00 PM

*On Saturdays leaves at 10.30 P. M. instead of 9.20 P. M. †On Saturdays leaves at 10.05 P. M. instead of 9.10 P.M.
‡All trains leave Tybee from 104th station, except on Sundays; the 4.30 P. M., 5.00 P. M., and 5.30 P. M. trains leave from Tybee
station and trains leaving 4.30 P. M., and 5.30 P. M. make no local stops. § Makes no local stops.
For additional information as to stops at local stations, consult Ticket Agent, or see newspapers and pocket schedule cards.

Trains Arrive and Depart at Tybee Depot, Randolph and President Streets

OIL BURNING ENGINES—NO CINDERS

CENTRAL OF GEORGIA RAILWAY

WM. B. CLEMENTS, City Passenger and Ticket Agent
37 Bull Street

The two large bodies of water that the Savannah-to-Tybee rail line had to cross were St. Augustine Creek and Lazaretto Creek. Substantial bridges, trestles, and causeways had to be built to cross these waterways. The above photograph shows a train crossing Lazaretto Creek. (Courtesy of the Tybee Island Historical Society.)

This mid-1920s photograph shows an automobile driving on Tybee Road alongside a Central of Georgia Railway Company passenger train as they both travel through Romerly Marsh. The road to Tybee Island opened on June 21, 1923. It became designated as US Route 80 in 1926 and runs all the way from San Diego, California, to Tybee Island. This road made Tybee Island an even greater attraction to tourists from all over the country, and it dramatically reduced the need to reach the island by ship or railroad. (Courtesy of the Georgia Historical Society.)

The train to Tybee Island was always affectionately known as the "Marsh Hen." It was very popular with Savannah-area residents as well as visiting tourists, making six or more trips daily during the busy summer season, from May to September, and a reduced schedule during the less busy off-season months. (Courtesy of the Tybee Island Historical Society.)

Central of Georgia Railway locomotive Engine No. 1560 is seen below at the end of the line on the Tybee turntable, which was located at the west end of today's Inlet Avenue on Tybee Island. The turntable allowed locomotive engines to be turned around for the return trip to Savannah. (Courtesy of Ed Mims.)

Central of Georgia Railway locomotive Engine No. 1558 can be seen in this 1915 photograph pulling freight cars at Tybee Island. Operations on the Central of Georgia Railway's Tybee Branch were not limited to passengers only. In 1910, for example, 8,614 tons of freight were hauled. Freight costs for groceries were charged at the rate of 50¢ per hundred pounds, beer and soft drinks at 35¢ per hundred pounds, and a half barrel of whiskey at the rate of $2.35. To bring in a carload of lumber, the charge was $10, and $40 per car was charged for other construction materials. (Courtesy of Ed Mims.)

Walter Boyd stands next to a Central of Georgia Railway locomotive engine. In the mid-1920s, approximately a quarter of a million passengers per year, hailing from many states in the Union, were transported to Tybee Island by the Central of Georgia Railway Company. Trains from Savannah to Tybee ran almost hourly during the busy summer months, and since Tybee trains had oil-burning engines, the 45-minute run to Tybee Depot was free from cinders, smoke, and dust. (Courtesy of the Tybee Island Historical Society.)

This advertisement appeared on the Central of Georgia Railway Company's Tybee excursion rates posters in 1908. Posters and booklets promoting travel to Tybee Island were produced and widely distributed by the Central of Georgia Railway Company throughout Georgia and Alabama. This attracted very large numbers of visitors to Tybee Island and caused it to rapidly develop into a very popular seaside resort destination. (Courtesy of the Central of Georgia Railway Historical Society.)

At left is another example of an advertisement that appeared on the Central of Georgia Railway Company's Tybee excursion rates posters in the early 1900s. In the mid-1920s, individual round-trip tickets from Savannah to Tybee were 50¢ for adults and 25¢ for children. By purchasing 50 round-trip tickets, the price was reduced to 18¢ per adult per trip. "Where Ocean Breezes Blow" was a popular advertising slogan used by the Central of Georgia on posters, timetables, and other promotional items to encourage travel to Tybee Island on its trains. Tybee advertisements often included a young woman in bathing attire appropriate for the era. Hotel Tybee can be seen in the background of this poster. (Courtesy of Ed Mims.)

123

TYBEE

Where Ocean Breezes Blow
More Beautiful and Attractive
Than Ever

LOW ROUND TRIP FARES

Sunday Only, Tickets $1.75
Week-End Tickets .. $4.50
10-Day Tickets $5.00
Season Tickets $7.35

Sunday Only Tickets on Sale for Train leaving
Augusta 6:50 a. m., Sundays.

Beginning Sunday, June 1, 1913.

ASK THE TICKET AGENT

Shown here is a 1913 advertisement promoting train travel to Tybee Island from Augusta, Georgia. Low excursion fares from many points in Georgia, Alabama, and other southeastern states during the busy summer season helped to make an annual Tybee vacation relatively inexpensive for most people. To reach Tybee, persons in Georgia and Alabama were able to ride the Central of Georgia Railway directly to Savannah and then connect to the Central of Georgia's Tybee Branch for the final segment of their journey to the beach. (Courtesy of Barry Paschal.)

An unidentified boy stands next to the front end of a Central of Georgia Railway Company's locomotive engine. An engineering marvel for that era, the Savannah-to-Tybee railroad line was built using surveys, maps, and diagrams drawn by prominent railroad engineer Capt. John Postell, and railroad contractor T.B. Inness was hired to construct the line. (Courtesy of the Tybee Island Historical Society.)

This boy and girl on roller skates stand in front of the Lovell train station on Tybee Island while waiting to catch the next train. The sign above their heads warns people to not jump on or off moving trains, which can be hazardous. (Courtesy of the Tybee Island Historical Society.)

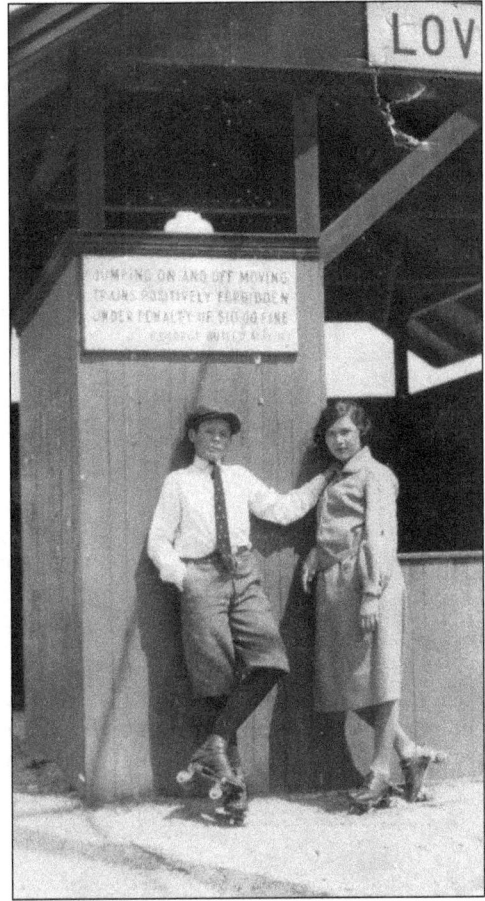

Central of Georgia Railway's Tybee Island depot is shown on this postcard, which was sent in the US Mail on April 8, 1912. The men are seen wearing suits and hats, and women are wearing full dresses. (Author's collection.)

Central of Georgia Depot, Tybee Beach,
Tybee Island, near Savannah, Ga.

Central of Georgia Depot, Tybee Beach.

Another, wider-angle view of Central of Georgia Railway's Tybee Island depot is shown on this postcard, which was produced around 1913. Many residents of polluted cities seeking refuge at the beach passed through this train depot. At the time, saltwater breezes were believed to be a remedy for various ailments, including asthma and numerous allergies. (Author's collection.)

Train at South End, Tybee Island, Ga.

This early-1900s postcard shows a Central of Georgia Railway passenger train at the south end of Tybee Island. Note the different types of wooden passenger cars, including the second car with a flat roof, likely one of the Central of Georgia's "suburban cars." (Author's collection.)

This postcard's photograph, which was taken on the day Tybee Road opened on June 21, 1923, shows how all roads (railroads and automobile roads) lead to Tybee Island. The Central of Georgia Railway Company, in the spirit of cooperation, contributed to the Tybee Road project a four-mile-long stretch of land along its own right-of-way. Ironically, it was the Tybee Road project for the benefit of automobiles that led to the decline in Tybee train ridership and ultimately to the demise of the Tybee Branch of the Central of Georgia Railway Company. (Courtesy of the Georgia Historical Society.)

This rare and grainy image shows the last train from Tybee Island before it departed on July 31, 1933. It consisted of eight wooden coaches carrying members of the Central of Georgia's Clerk's Organization picnic. It is shown here at the south end of Tybee Island prior to being turned on the turntable for the final trip to Savannah. The crew for the last train consisted of conductor G.C. Hitt, engineer H.L. Zeigler, flagman J.W. Sasser, and fireman J.T. Ryle. (Courtesy of the Central of Georgia Railway Historical Society.)

127

Visit us at
arcadiapublishing.com

www.ingramcontent.com/pod-product-compliance
Lightning Source LLC
Chambersburg PA
CBHW050635110426

42813CB00007B/1819